A Ragged Mountain Press
WOMAN'S GUIDE

# CLIMBING

## SHELLEY PRESSON

### Series Editor, Molly Mulhern Gross

RAGGED MOUNTAIN PRESS / McGRAW-HILL

Camden, Maine • New York • San Francisco • Washington, D.C. • Auckland
Bogotá • Caracas • Lisbon • London • Madrid • Mexico City • Milan
Montreal • New Delhi • San Juan • Singapore • Sydney • Tokyo • Toronto

# Look for these other Ragged Mountain Press Woman's Guides

*Backpacking*, Adrienne Hall
*Canoeing*, Laurie Gullion
*Fly-Fishing*, Dana Rikimaru
*Golf*, Susan Comolli
*Mountaineering*, Andrea Gabbard
*Powerboating*, Sandy Lindsey

*Sailing*, Doris Colgate
*Scuba Diving*, Claire Walter
*Sea Kayaking*, Shelley Johnson
*Skiing*, Maggie Loring
*Snowboarding*, Julia Carlson
*Winter Sports*, Iseult Devlin

• • • • • • • • • • • • • • • • • • • • • • • • • • • • • • • •

## Ragged Mountain Press
### A Division of The McGraw-Hill Companies

10 9 8 7 6 5 4 3 2 1
Copyright © 2000 Shelley Presson
Foreword © 2000 Molly Mulhern Gross

All rights reserved. The publisher takes no responsibility for the use of any of the materials or methods described in this book, nor for the products thereof. The name "Ragged Mountain Press" and the Ragged Mountain Press logo are trademarks of The McGraw-Hill Companies. Printed in the United States of America.

*Library of Congress Cataloging-in-Publication Data*

Presson, Shelley.
    Climbing / Shelley Presson.
        p.    cm.—(A Ragged Mountain Press woman's guide)
    Includes bibliographical references and index.
    ISBN 0-07-135151-5 (alk. paper)
    1. Rock climbing. 2. Women rock climbers. I. Title.
    II. Series

GV200.P74 2000
796.52'2'082—dc21                                00-24814

Questions regarding the content of this book should be addressed to
Ragged Mountain Press
P.O. Box 220
Camden, ME 04843
http://www.raggedmountainpress.com

Questions regarding the ordering of this book should be addressed to
The McGraw-Hill Companies
Customer Service Department
P.O. Box 547
Blacklick, OH 43004
Retail customers: 1-800-262-4729
Bookstores: 1-800-722-4726

This book is printed on 70# Citation.

Printed by Quebecor Printing Company, Fairfield, PA
Design by Carol Inouye, Inkstone Communications Design
Production management by Janet Robbins
Page layout by Shannon Thomas
Edited by Shana Harrington

Illustrations by Elayne Sears
Photos courtesy of Andrew Dunbar unless otherwise indicated:
Pages 66, 123, and 165, courtesy Greg Epperson; pages 12–13, 14, 23, 29, 67, 89 (left), 101, and 139, courtesy Stewart M. Green; page 27 courtesy Pat Kelly; page 20 courtesy Kate Lapides; pages 16, 34, 36, 38, 41, 69, 75, 89 (right), 95, 100, 106 (top left), 144 (top right), 155, and 164 courtesy Cliff Leight; page 87 courtesy Cliff Leight/Enchantments; pages 35, 39, 136, and 142 courtesy Metolius; pages 48, 128 (center), and 131 courtesy Petzl; page 158 courtesy Yaroslav Pogozhev; pages 32, 84, 85 (bottom), 88 (top right), 90 (top right), 93, 120, and 157 courtesy Corey Rich; page 156 courtesy Corey Rich/Lee Haus/Made in the Shade; page 47 courtesy Cheyenne Rouse; pages 85 (top), 109 (bottom), 159 and 161 courtesy Jorge Visser; and page 18 courtesy Beth Wald.

Advil, Band-Aid, DoubleBack, Gjust Tibloc, Grigri, Lycra, Motrin, Sport Cord, Velcro, and Women That Rock are registered trademarks.

WARNING: This is an instructional book for potentially dangerous activities. Rock climbing, ice climbing, and mountaineering may subject you to climbing falls; rock and ice fall; frostbite and hypothermia; drowning; and many other hazards that can lead to serious injury and death.

Brand-name items of equipment mentioned or shown in this book are for purposes of illustration or discussion only and do not constitute a recommendations for their use.

This book is not intended to replace instruction by a qualified instructor nor to substitute for your personal judgement.

In using this book, the reader releases the author, publisher, and distributor from liability for any injury, including death, that might result.

•••••••••••••••••••••••••••••

"**T**hrough climbing I discovered
a woman that I did not know
was inside me."

—Hollie Vargas, climbing gym manager

•••••••••••••••••••••••••••••

# Foreword

**A** few years ago I purchased a climbing guide to a local cliff, curious to see why a sheer outcropping I'd seen from my kayak appealed to climbers. I was no climber, and had no idea what those spider-like folk were up to. The book wasn't much help, filled with exotically named routes (Templeton's Crack and Slow Children) carrying even stranger numbers (5.11c, 5.10a, NEI4+). Not long after I purchased the book I began hiking around boulders at the base of these same cliffs. One day I even took my kids—we played a game of finding all the chalk marks left on the boulders by sweaty climber's hands, intermittently craning our necks up the cliff to watch the odd bodies dangling in space.

I'm drawn to the these cliffs partially for their immense beauty, partially for the challenge of getting up them. I knew I wasn't magically going to ascend those cliffs, so eventually I enrolled in a climbing course at the local YMCA. I took the climbing class with my best buddy. Two nights a week we met at the wall, two mid-thirtyish moms looking for a diversion from the daily grind. Somedays we'd push each other to do speed climbs. Other days we'd put on blindfolds to climb by feel instead of look. I remember the awe at the power of my arms and legs, the throbbing sensation of being pumped, the exhilaration of getting to the top and realizing that my fear of heights had been overcome. Those nights were rejuvenating.

But it was a revelation I had as I poured water into a coffee pot one morning that really convinced me what climbing was about. As I stood and watched the cold clear water flow from jug to pot—witnessing the strength and clarity of motion that only water flowing clearly, fluidily, flawlessly suggests—I recognized the feeling that overcame my body as it worked itself across the climbing wall. It was a state of flow: clear, concentrated effort to get from point a to point b. It's a feeling I've never had before, not in running, swimming or snowboarding. Climbing requires a concentration and unity of mind with muscle that culminates in a state I can only liken to running water. Flow. It's yours once you place yourself up on that wall or that crag. And once you've felt it—concentrated so hard and moved with such precision that a millimeter position change in your toe is the difference between pushing to the next height or slipping off the wall—you'll want more.

*Climbing: A Woman's Guide* is designed to help you begin to experience that flow. We've designed this guide to be especially easy to use, full of encouragement, advice, and sound technical information. We've done our best to mimic the learning conditions of a woman's instructional clinic.

What's so different about the way women learn? If you're like me, you want to hear a description of a method or tactic before launching into it. I'm a fan of the talk-it-over-and-think-it-through-first school of learning. I prefer to ask questions *before* I'm asked to belay my best friend on the neighborhood climbing wall. And I like to learn in a group so I can hear other folks' questions—

and know I'm not the only one wondering how to tie a figure 8 knot or clip on a carabiner (see pages 72–73 and 130!). Here you'll find lots of women's voices: your instructor's, of course, but also voices of women from all walks of life who love the outdoors. There's a sense of camaraderie, honesty, and just plain fun. *Climbing: A Woman's Guide* provides solutions, advice, and stories from women who have done what you are about to do: learn to climb.

I hope Shelley's words and approach help get you out climbing and enjoying. I'll look for you out there. Between climbing trips, drop us a note to tell us how we're doing and how we can improve these guides to best suit you and your learning style.

MOLLY MULHERN GROSS
Series Editor, The Ragged Mountain Press Woman's Guides
Camden, Maine

*An avid outdoorswoman, Molly Mulhern Gross enjoys running, hiking, camping, sea kayaking, telemark skiing, in-line skating, biking, and snowboarding. She is Director of Editing, Design, and Production at Ragged Mountain Press and International Marine.*

# CONTENTS

 **CONTENTS**

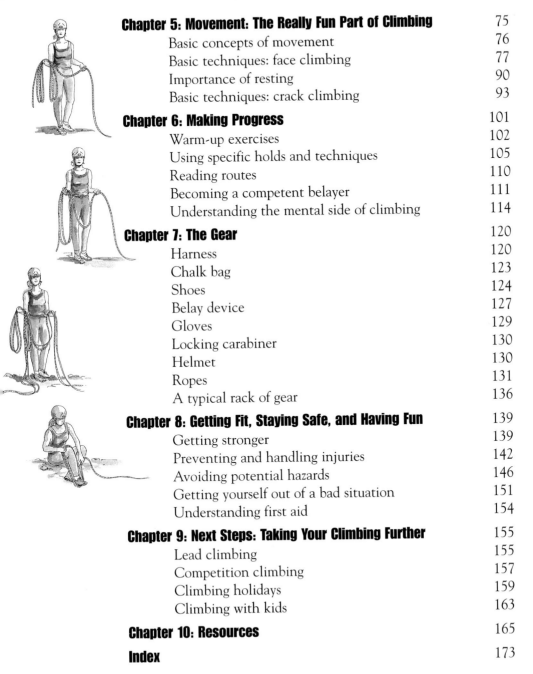

# Acknowledgments

Throughout the experience of writing of this book I became keenly aware that this was not an individual endeavor but the convergence of the ideas, the support, the knowledge and the inspiration of many people in my life.

Thanks to Mark Hudon for teaching me to climb. Without his early influence on the importance of technique, I would not be the climber I am today, nor would I have been asked to write a book like this.

A very special thanks to all the women who generously took the time to write down their personal experiences in climbing, which so perfectly illustrate so many passages in this book. A special acknowledgment (and apology) goes to Sue Patenaude for her personal account to me of her early climbing experiences, which reinforced many of my ideas. Unfortunately, as I didn't have the heart to edit her brilliantly written narrative, none of her words ended up in these pages. And to all the women who have taken my clinics over the years: thanks for teaching me so much about teaching and for being so excited about the sport. Your struggles and triumphs, and your woman's perspective were a terrific inspiration.

Many thanks are also due to Molly Mulhern Gross for coming up with the Ragged Mountain Press Woman's Guides and for asking me to author this one. I am especially grateful for the support, guidance, and patience that Molly, D. A. Oliver, and Janet Robbins gave me throughout. I am proud and appreciative of having such a unique format for introducing women to this sport I love so much.

I also owe this accomplishment (like all others in my life) to my family for instilling in me the belief that I can do *anything* I set my sights on.

And finally, to my husband, Andrew Dunbar, whose support and strength were with me every step of the way: Thank you for believing in me, enduring my fits of perfectionism, taking over when I just got too overwhelmed and for loving me even when I wasn't very lovable.

# Introduction

I recall vividly my introduction to rock climbing. It was a book that inspired me. In fact, until I saw that book, I didn't even know what rock climbing was. I suppose I must have had a vague notion that people climbed big mountains like Everest, but I didn't really grasp what that meant or how one might get started in such a superhuman endeavor. Considering that I'd never done *anything* athletic in my life until age 19, it's no wonder I didn't conceive of such a thing as rock climbing.

At that point, my only experience with sports was running, which I had taken up in college to lose weight and had subsequently become obsessed with, and skiing, which I had tried because I was working in a ski shop. Because I'd never done *any* sports as a kid, I was absolutely fanatic about both sports. I felt I had a lot of catching up to do.

One year in the spring, when ski season was nearing an end, some of the guys from the shop asked me whether I'd like to try rock climbing. (They had witnessed my introduction to skiing, so they knew I was keen to try new sports.) My reaction was something like, "Yeah! . . . Uh, what is it?" That's when they showed me a book called *Learning to Rock Climb*.

The book was mostly a photo gallery of movements and techniques, and the climber demonstrating the movements was a woman. I was absolutely taken by the idea—somehow, as I perused the photos, I sensed that I could do what the woman in the photos was doing. Her movements and body positions reminded me of positions I had encountered in modern dance classes I had taken in high school. Something just clicked. That week after poring over the book, I arranged to go to the local climbing area with one of the guys from the shop. I was so certain that this sport was for me that the day before we were to go—and without having ever climbed—I bought a pair of climbing shoes and a *harness* (a belt- and leg-loop combination made of nylon webbing that is worn by the climber to secure her to the climbing rope). A big investment for a struggling student (and not one I necessarily recommend for those who haven't climbed at least once!).

That first time out changed my life forever. It was like nothing I had ever done before, and it was so beyond *anything* that I perceived I was capable of doing. From that day on, all I could think about was climbing. My obsession was so great, it was a miracle I graduated from college. After college, much to my parents' chagrin, I became a full-time climber, traveling the world to do what I loved. That focus led to competitions, sponsorship, TV commercials, photo shoots, and later teaching clinics on climbing technique and movement throughout the United States.

In my "women-only" clinics, I explained how climbing had changed my life: I had been a timid, uncoordinated, nonathletic girl, and if *I* could do it, anyone could. Climbing had given me confidence and insight into my own natural abilities, abilities I didn't know I had. I was determined to help break down the myths about climbing and help women find their own undiscovered strengths and talents. I shared my fears, my self-doubts, and my weaknesses as well as how I overcame those hurdles. I taught the women things about movement that it had taken me years to "get," and I showed them as many "tricks" as I could that would propel them past their plateaus. The responses from the women floored me. They were so excited to know this stuff, to realize that they, too, could do this sport and succeed in it. Every time I finished a clinic, I felt a tremendous reward; however clichéd it may sound, I felt I was giving something back to this sport that had given me so much.

And yet, I often finished my clinics feeling also as if I had only skimmed the surface, that there was so much more that I could have given the participants. Time was always the limiting factor. With only three to four hours and 10 to 15 women in a clinic, there was simply no way I could transmit my 16 years of climbing experience in any effective way for all skill levels. I also realized, from talking to women after the clinics or to women I would encounter in gyms or at the crags, that there was no comprehensive source of answers for the questions or concerns that women climbers might have.

So when the idea of writing a book about climbing for women presented itself, I remembered that it was a book that had given me the inspiration to try this sport. I also felt that if a book like the one you're reading now had existed when I started, it would have shortened my learning curve. Although climbing had captured my imagination immediately, and although that book with the photos of the woman helped encourage me, there were years of learning, failure, frustration, and heartache in my road to becoming a competent climber. I also realized that a book of photos couldn't have shown me any of the mental or emotional hurdles I would encounter or the specific challenges a woman faces getting started in the sport.

## WHAT IS CLIMBING?

The word *climbing* encompasses many different types of activities: mountaineering, ice climbing, alpine climbing, bouldering, traditional gear climbing, and sport climbing. All of these activities are subsports within the sport called *climbing*. These subsports were started by the first climbers, who were really *mountaineers* (climbers who are mainly interested in reaching the summits of mountains and peaks, which entails climbing ice, walking over snowfields and glaciers, as well as climbing rock). To climb and conquer the summits of the major mountains of the world, mountaineers "practiced" the different elements they would encounter in their grand expeditions. They would practice rock climbing, for example, at lesser altitudes and on cliffs nearer to home. Of course, they found a great deal of joy and satisfaction in these "practice" activities, and they came to pursue them just as much as they pursued climbing big mountains.

For this book, we'll be talking about *rock climbing* specifically, although we're going to drop the word *rock* and mostly just refer to the activity as *climbing*. (Climbers themselves usually call it *climbing*, because it can be done on rock or on artificial climbing walls and because it's the most practiced of the subsports.) In climbing, you choose a path up a wall and use both your hands and your feet on the irregularities and features to make upward progress. Sometimes the goal is to go up 5 feet, sometimes to go up 500. Your progress depends on balance, agility, strength, judgment, problem solving, and the ability to keep a calm and relaxed head in the midst of tenuous positions.

Because there is some inherent risk, the sport demands that climbers be intensely focused on the medium, the strategy, and the safety systems. A climber must be mentally, physically, and even emotionally present—there is no room for worrying about that project at work, the late house payment, or that funny noise your brakes are making. It is this complete focus, these few moments of being in that place that some climbers call "the zone," that attracts people to climbing.

## ABOUT THIS BOOK

In this book I take a step-by-step approach to getting started and progressing in climbing. I begin with the assumption that you've never climbed, and I cover in detail what you'll need to know to have a smooth and safe start in this sport. I present the information in a way that should mirror your experience as you progress from complete novice to an advanced climber, so you will feel comfortable and relaxed with each new experience.

Throughout the book, I address the mental and psychological aspects of the sport because at least 90 percent of your success will be because of what's in your head rather than what you do with your body or your gear. I start off with some of the common concerns and then move to the types of climbing so you will have a good understanding of what you're getting into. I cover in depth how and where you can get started, what gear you'll be using and how to know what's right for you, how the safety systems work, and what you can expect when you fall.

Although the book is designed to get you started, I go beyond the basics in the chapters on movement, improving your skills, buying gear, and staying fit and safe. This is meant to be a book that you'll be able to reference no matter what level you attain in climbing. I've also included voices of other women climbers, from the novice to the world-class, to give you some alternative perspectives and to inspire you.

With that said, I must also express to you that no book, even an educational book such as this, can replace the actual experience of climbing. You absolutely will need to follow up reading this book by learning the ropes (pun intended) from a professional instructor or an experienced friend—no book can replace that kind of instruction. You should also be aware that without having climbed before, you may not "get" everything the first read. Don't worry if you don't grasp a certain concept or if you can't picture a certain technique I describe. It will all come together once you actually begin climbing.

# Chapter 1

# WHO CAN CLIMB?

There is something very captivating about climbing. Perhaps it's the improbability of the sport itself: human beings hanging spider-like from their hands and feet on the side of a rock, working their way upward on imaginary holds on a face. It's intriguing and mysterious. Many observers gaze up at climbers and wonder, "How do they do that?"

For newcomers, the sport can also be intimidating. Many women who have never climbed have an impression that it is a macho sport, a sport where burly muscles and fearlessness are mandatory. I often hear women express doubts about whether they can do it, whether they are strong enough, or whether they would be simply too scared to try.

Maybe you wonder whether you have what it takes to be a climber. Perhaps a little background about me might help.

Not long ago a feature story on me was run on the front page of the sports section of my hometown newspaper, the *Sacramento Bee*. A few weeks later I received a letter from a man who had been my sixth-grade teacher and later one of my twelfth-grade teachers as well. As I read his letter, I began to cry.

My teacher wrote to say that he had seen the article and had recognized me as a former student. He had been prompted to write because he was so amazed that the puny, timid, uncoordinated Shelley Presson had become a top rock climber. He wrote, "You were the last person I would have

● ● ● ● ● ● ● ● ● ● ● ● ● ● ● ● ● ● ● ● ● ● ● ● ● ● ●

**Y**ou don't have to be exceptionally strong, nor do you have to be especially bold or courageous.

● ● ● ● ● ● ● ● ● ● ● ● ● ● ● ● ● ● ● ● ● ● ● ● ● ● ●

This climber is showing good form by focusing on footwork and balance instead of using her arms to make upward progress.

*ever* guessed would have gone on to achieve success in this way." He didn't say it in a mean-spirited way, but more out of wonder and curiosity.

Most people who knew me growing up would have thought the same thing. Like a lot of women my age, I didn't do any sports as a kid. I was pretty much considered a wimp—mostly because I was a small, weak child. And as a child does, I took to heart the very clear messages from my peers and teachers and I let those messages dictate my own perception: I wasn't athletic, and so I should just forget about doing *any* sports. And, of course, as the cliché goes, I didn't get picked for anybody's team.

I'm telling you this because maybe you have the impression that to climb you must have tremendous strength or you must be one of those "natural athletes." Many women wonder whether they have what it takes physically to climb. On top of that is the mental fear: climbing can be pretty daunting at first glance (I'll talk in depth about this fear in the following chapter). That's why I am so excited to share with you a simple truth: you don't have to be exceptionally strong, nor do you have to be especially bold or courageous—I am neither.

## A GOOD MATCH FOR WOMEN

We'll talk about the physical part first. Do you have to be a "natural athlete"? You already are! At least for climbing, anyway. One of the most intriguing and unexpected discoveries I made in my early days of teaching and doing clinics was that women are actually *better beginner climbers than men are*. I don't mean to sound sexist, but there are several reasons women naturally excel at climbing. (Of course, this is a rash generalization, and I've encountered both men and women who don't represent this theory.)

●     **Climbing requires balance and grace**. Women seem to find their balance over their feet more readily than men do. This may have something to do with our lower center of gravity. More women have been involved with dance, ballet, gymnastics, or yoga and so are way ahead when it comes to moving with grace and maintaining their balance.

- **Climbing is not a muscle sport; it's a technique sport**. Good technique in climbing is all in the feet, the hips, and the body position—not in the arms. When a guy climbs for the first few times, he tends to pull himself up the wall with his arms. This is because men naturally have more muscle in their upper body, so they are more inclined to use it. In contrast, women don't typically have a lot of strength in their upper bodies and, therefore, *cannot* rely on their arms to get them up the climb. By default, women will use their feet and legs to push them up the wall, a practice that also happens to be a better technique.

- **Climbing is not as natural as it may seem**. Women are great listeners. This is important in learning to climb, because often your instructor's words will go against what your human instinct is telling you. Women tend to follow direction better and have an easier time trusting people (in this case, the instructor).

- **Climbing isn't about being aggressive**. It is important to read the sequence of movement in climbing, to grip the holds gently, and to know how to relax and trust your feet and your sense of balance. These are things that women beginners take to much more naturally than do men.

Climber in a gymnastic position, Shelf Road, Colorado.

## WHAT YOU'LL GET FROM CLIMBING AND WHY IT MIGHT CHANGE YOUR LIFE

Once you get out there climbing—once you learn the safety techniques and what the gear does and once you realize what your body and mind are capable of—you'll experience changes that affect your whole life. Here are some ways climbing could change your life:

- **Climbing is a fantastic way to stay fit and lean**. Climbers naturally develop a great strength-to-body-weight ratio. When you're climbing, you use muscles you didn't even know you had; the result is that your overall muscle tone improves.

On top of that, I've found that many women have noticed an increase in their metabolisms, which is most likely due to their overall increase in muscle.

- **Climbing can increase your confidence and self-esteem**. You cannot imagine the thrill and the satisfaction you get from climbing something that had seemed so impossible and so far beyond your capabilities. Once you realize that you *can* do this sport, you will look at yourself in a different light. It gives you a mental edge in many situations. I've found that women begin to believe in their own abilities more. This new perspective breeds an attitude of "I can climb, so I can do anything." And, in fact, because climbing is perceived as

Focusing intently on the next hold; nothing else matters.

such an improbable sport, especially for women, you gain a tremendous amount of confidence because you have achieved something you may have thought wasn't possible.

Hollie Vargas, manager of Vertical Relief climbing gym in Flagstaff, Arizona, says: "Through climbing I discovered a woman that I did not know was inside me. By pushing myself just a little harder than I thought I could, making one more move up or doing a climb I didn't think I could, I realized that I had the potential to push through other things in life that I didn't think I could do. As a matter of fact, I think climbing inspired me to go to graduate school, something I never thought I would do."

- **Climbing can teach you how to manage stress, how to focus, and how to relax when things get crazy.** Climbing demands focus, relaxation, and calm reactions in the midst of pretty intense situations. As you progress in climbing, you will develop the skills to relax and focus when the pressure is on. Of course, once you have these skills, you'll find that they work in *any* stressful situation. Your mental muscles become just as honed as your physical muscles.

• • • • • • • • • • • • • • • • • • • • • • • • •

"Through climbing I discovered a woman that I did not know was inside me."

—Hollie Vargas, climbing gym manager

• • • • • • • • • • • • • • • • • • • • • • • • •

Climbing can help you recapture the joy of being a kid.

**Climbing is simply incredibly fun!** It's like being a kid again. Climbing takes our bodies and minds back to a time before we were afraid, when we climbed trees and fences and just about anything—because we could. Who knows where our instinct to climb comes from, but nearly every kid does it naturally. Eventually, usually because of a bad fall, our desire to climb is curbed. Then, as adults, we become cognizant of the consequences of falling, and the climbing instinct is killed—almost. But once a person takes climbing up again, the joy and spontaneity of it become addictive.

## HOW AND WHY THEY GOT STARTED

### From the sidelines into the action

About eight years ago, just out of college, Rebecca Rusch went to work at a fancy Chicago health club that had a 100-foot climbing wall. Even though she had participated in sports during school, without formal athletics she was bored and lacked motivation. As she worked, Rebecca would watch countless people trying to claw their way to the top. She was intrigued with how focused they were, seemingly oblivious to the pounding aerobics music or the other members of the club staring at them. Rebecca remembers, "They just seemed to want so badly to get to the top of that piece of plastic. Few of them made it, but they kept trying, which made me curious to try it as well."

After a while Rebecca got the courage to give it a go. She says, "I was intimidated and scared, but I swallowed my pride and started clawing my way up. I only made it about 30 feet, but I was more engrossed during those 30 feet than I had been in a very long time. I came down exhilarated and laughing. Little did I know that day would change my life, and climbing would become an integral part in everything I do."

For Rebecca, learning to climb sparked a fleeting desire that had always been there but was hidden under societal and family expectations of school, work, and so on. About a year after learning to climb she took a three-month climbing road trip to California.

"I was in heaven! Exploring, climbing almost every day, sleeping in the dirt. My climbing was improving, but more importantly, I was learning about myself. As the trip drew to a close, I didn't want to return to the 'real world.' So I didn't. I stayed in California and soon got jobs as an outdoor climbing instructor and a salesperson in an outdoor sports store. I became immersed in climbing. From there, climbing partners and opportunities kept opening up for me. It made me realize that I could build a life around what I loved to do, blurring the line between my career and my outdoor passion." Rebecca Rusch, at 31, is now part owner of Rockreation climbing gym, climbing instructor, and adventure racer.

## Climbing past self-doubt

Hilary Harris, of Boulder, Colorado, has been climbing for 10 years. She was one of the first—and remains one of the very few—women to climb V9 in bouldering (see page 40 for bouldering difficulty ratings), and she has climbed all over the world. She began climbing during her freshman year in college.

Hilary remembers: "When I started climbing, I had very low self-esteem—I wasn't doing well in school, I was involved in drugs, I was overweight, and I was in an unhealthy relationship. At first, climbing was just another thing that I could consume to fill some need I couldn't define. I guess I thought I'd be cool if I looked like a climber. I remember literally worshipping climbers I saw in magazines and thinking they had something that I didn't. After climbing for about a year, I confided my dreams of climbing a 5.11 to a friend of mine. He asked me, 'Why just 5.11? Why not 5.12 or 5.13?' My incredulous response was, 'Only awesome people can do that!' His next words helped me to begin to question my own self-doubt: 'What makes you think you're not awesome too?' I began to set my sights much higher and achieved things in climbing I hadn't dreamed were possible. I learned a lot about myself and what I was capable of. Climbing taught me how to be visionary. It taught me the values of hard work, perseverance, patience, and courage. It taught me how limiting self-perception can be. But most of all, it taught me to believe in myself."

• • • • • • • • • • • • • • • • • • • • • • • • • • • • • • • • • • • • • • • • • • • • • • • • • •

"Climbing taught me how to be visionary. It taught me the values of hard work, perseverance, patience, and courage. It taught me how limiting self-perception can be. But most of all, it taught me to believe in myself."

—Hilary Harris, Boulder, Colorado

• • • • • • • • • • • • • • • • • • • • • • • • • • • • • • • • • • • • • • • • • • • • • • • • • •

## A LEGEND IN CLIMBING

Lynn Hill

Lynn Hill is the most recognized climber—female or male—in the world. When you first meet her, you can't help but notice how small she is. At 5 feet, 2 inches, Lynn is quite short even for a woman. The second thing you notice are her intense blue eyes. Lynn's fame dates back to the 1970s when she was pushing the standards of traditional climbing; in the 1980s she was always on the podium in World Cup competitions, and in the 1990s she did something that no other climber in the world had done. In 1993 Lynn free climbed a route on El Capitan called the Nose, which had previously been climbed only by using aid techniques. She was on the 3,000-foot wall for two days. For years, the best climbers in the world—all of them men at that time—had tried it, but no one had succeeded. In 1994, she went back to do the route again in a one-day ascent. Lynn views her achievement as a contribution and a statement to all climbers: "Whatever size, whatever body type you are, you can achieve great things with a strong belief and conviction."

Interviewed by Kathleen Gasperini for MountainZone.com ("Going to Extremes," ©1998) during filming of a large-format movie featuring Lynn climbing in the Canyonlands, Lynn related this story that tells much about her early beliefs about gender in climbing: "When I was 14 years old, I was bouldering in Joshua Tree and trying to overcome a mantle problem that required a certain amount of strength to push your weight up and over. This guy came over and said, 'Gee, I can't even do that.' I thought, well, why would you expect that you automatically could do it? Just because I was a small girl, was I not going to be able to do it? It was a memorable experience because it occurred to me then that other people had a different view of what I should or shouldn't be capable of doing. I think that people should just do whatever they can do or want to do. It shouldn't be a matter of if they're a man or a woman; it shouldn't be a matter of one's sex. And climbing, fortunately, is a sport that's great for women. It includes a certain combination of grace and power and psychological aspects. You can use your own attributes to be a great climber."

### Age not a factor

At the age of 57, Diane La Duca decided that she was going to rid herself of the "life-is-all-down-hill-after-menopause" programming. She took a class called Fight Gravity at a climbing gym in Costa Mesa, California. As a result, Diane says, "I found a whole new wellness and strength in climbing that I hadn't felt in years."

Diane was so excited that she urged her friend Patricia Kelly, 60, to take the class "in order to get over her fear of heights." Patricia's fear of heights was such that she was reluctant even to climb a ladder to change a light bulb. According to Patricia, "Since I am a spiritual counselor and meditation teacher, I decided it was time for me to walk my talk and clear this debilitating fear

• • • • • • • • • • • • • • • • • • • • • • • • • •

"**W**e always push gently
against the edges of our fear
and always remember to
have a good time."

—Diane La Duca and Patricia Kelly,
new climbers at ages 57 and 60

• • • • • • • • • • • • • • • • • • • • • • • • • •

Pat and Diane's enthusiasm and love of the sport are impressive. They're an inspiration to young and old alike!

from my own space." In that first class, Patricia got on the wall three or four times and made it about 15 feet off the ground before asking to be lowered. It was a start.

Diane herself was really jazzed about climbing and bought memberships at the gym for both of them. Diane did most of the climbing, but once in a while Patricia would climb a little. Gradually she noticed that she was climbing higher and higher each time, until one day she reached the top.

That was three and a half years ago. The two women have since started climbing outside and have even done several multi-pitch climbs at places like Joshua Tree, Tahquitz, and Suicide Rock in California. They have a strategy they share when people marvel at their starting so late in this sport: "We always push gently against the edges of our fear and always remember to have a good time." Diane La Duca and Patricia Kelly both live in southern California and get out nearly every weekend.

# Chapter 2

# COMMON CONCERNS AND FEARS

**I** fall nearly *every* time I climb —I figure you're not pushing yourself if you're not falling.

**B**ecause rock climbing is so often misunderstood or misrepresented, common fears and apprehensions prevent some people from even trying the sport. For example, you might believe that climbers must be both fearless and super gutsy or thin as a reed and strong as an ox—neither of which is true. Some have never tried the sport because they believe that if the climber falls, she dies (or at least gets seriously injured). *Nobody* wants to try a sport if they think the result of a mistake is death. People who don't climb often ask me such questions as "What if you fall?" or "Aren't you afraid of getting hurt (or worse)?" My answers usually surprise them: I fall nearly *every* time I climb—I figure you're not pushing yourself if you're not falling. This is not what nonclimbers expect to hear because they don't know that the ropes and safety systems are to keep us safe (and alive) *when* we fall. In this book, you'll learn about what we do as climbers to make our sport safe and to miminize risk. But before we get into all that, I feel it's important to address these misperceptions as well as other concerns you may have that might be getting in the way of your pursuit of this sport. I've found that most of the apprehensions people have about climbing stem from lack of knowledge or outright misinformation. Both of these can create self-limiting perceptions about whether or not you're cut out

• • • • • • • • • • • • • • • • • • • • • • • • • • • • •

"I feel fear almost every time I climb. It is a healthy, self-preserving emotion that shouldn't be squelched."

—Rebecca Rusch, 31, climbing instructor

• • • • • • • • • • • • • • • • • • • • • • • • • • • • •

for this sport, so I've included this chapter to educate, enlighten, and hopefully dispel any misinformation you might have.

Rebecca Rusch, 31, part owner of Rockreation climbing gym, climbing instructor, and adventure racer, says: "Sometimes people say to me, 'I can't climb; I am afraid of heights' or 'You are so brave to climb the things you do.' My response to these types of comments is that I am also afraid of heights and am a big chicken. I feel fear almost every time I climb. It is a healthy, self-preserving emotion that shouldn't be squelched. However, if you let your fear get out of control, it can affect your climbing in a negative way, causing you to overgrip or make rash, unsafe decisions. I have found that for me good preparation and knowledge of the climb help me rationalize and control my fears."

The rest of this chapter provides answers to the most common concerns I've heard from women over the years, along with ideas for overcoming them.

## I DON'T THINK I'M STRONG ENOUGH TO CLIMB

One of the greatest myths about climbing is that you need to have strong arm and back muscles. It's easy to understand this misapprehension: what a nonclimber sees in the mainstream media are images of climbers dangling upside-down, orangutan-style, or hanging footless from giant overhanging roofs. Remember, some of what you've seen

**Top:** Climber recovering from a fall **Above:** Strong legs and determination are more important than upper-body strength.

may be sensationalism. Yet so much of climbing—especially what most climbers start out doing— is about how you use your feet and your legs and how you stay in balance. Think of how you climb a ladder: your hands and arms are usually just for balance, while your legs do the "climbing." Think about it: you would never attempt to climb a ladder without using your legs.

• • • • • • • • • • • • • • • • • • • • • • • • • • •

"I had already climbed a hard 5.10 when I finally did my first pull-up!"

—Cindy Knowles, art director, Atlanta, GA

• • • • • • • • • • • • • • • • • • • • • • • • • •

Initially in this sport, women have an advantage over men: a woman's legs are stronger, in a strength-to-body-weight sense, than a man's. If you start out on climbs that are easy enough, you should be using your legs to push you up the climb and you will actually need very little upper body strength. If you do feel that your arms aren't strong enough, you're probably on routes that are too hard or you simply need to be using your feet and legs more. As you progress into harder-rated climbs, the necessary strength will develop.

Cindy Knowles, 28, an art director in Atlanta, Georgia, remembers: "When I first began climbing I had pencil-like arms; I couldn't do a pull-up until I'd been climbing for three years. Fortunately, I had someone teaching me who focused on the importance of good footwork and technique, so I learned to use my feet, instead of pulling myself up with my arms. I had already climbed a hard 5.10 [see page 40] when I finally did my first pull-up! It shows how irrelevant that type of strength is for climbing."

## ALL OF THE CLIMBERS I SEE LOOK LIKE STICK FIGURES . . . BUT I'M HEAVYSET!

It's true that most climbers—especially those who have been climbing for a while—are on the leaner side. However, in most cases, they probably got that way *because* of climbing. Climbing is a sport that burns a lot of calories and, without really trying, you end up losing weight. The question is, can you start climbing even if you're overweight? The answer is a qualified "yes": if you can climb stairs or climb a ladder, then you can rock climb.

A more experienced climber demonstrates the opening moves to a friend who's just learning.

As I mentioned earlier in this chapter, climbing is about technique, balance, and footwork. In the beginning, the climbs you do will be at a low angle, so you will be (or should be) using your legs to push you up the climb and using your hands for balance. Even if you're carrying a few extra pounds, you should be able to rely on your legs for most of the movement. Of course, if you like climbing and stay with it, it's very likely you'll lose weight along the way.

Mi Sun Go, a Korean woman in her early thirties, began climbing as a way to lose weight. In less than one year she had lost 40 pounds. She loved climbing so much and was spending so much time doing it that she didn't really have to diet. The increase in exercise and muscle mass simply increased her metabolism. Of course, as she lost weight, her climbing improved, which in turn increased her motivation in the sport. Mi Sun Go is now the number one Korean competitive climber, and she was ranked 10th in the world in 1998.

Mi Sun Go, Korean National Champion

## MY FAMILY IS WORRIED THAT I'LL GET HURT. WHAT CAN I TELL THEM?

In the world of nonclimbers, there are many myths about climbing. Most of the misinformation has come from the (mostly exaggerated) images of climbing that the mainstream media presents. For some reason—possibly that climbing, as we really practice it, just isn't that exciting—the media portrays climbers as daredevils who narrowly escape death or who sometimes do not escape it if their equipment breaks or if they fall. The boring truth is that (1) our equipment almost never fails, and when it does it's usually due to operator error rather than some inherent flaw or weakness, and (2) we *do* fall, but the result is almost never death because of the safety techniques and equipment that we employ to protect us. Ho-hum.

What you and your family need to know is what really happens in climbing—not what's on TV. Climbers use such equipment as harnesses, ropes, *carabiners* (metal "snap links" used in safety systems), and belay devices as part of their safety systems. What you will learn in the beginning, before you ever leave the ground, is how to be safe and protected in the case of a fall. And you *will* fall. All climbers fall, but it is the *belay* (the safety system in which the climber's fall is held by the rope through a friction device) that keeps the fall from being dangerous. Later I present the details of the safety system and how to use it. Also, once you have actually gone climbing, you'll have a much easier time explaining to your loved ones how the safety system works.

You may also want to show your family some climbing magazines (or even this book) so that they can see that we use equipment and practice safe climbing. Here's a sample of some of the common myths about climbing and the ways that I've found to explain our sport to the nonclimbing world.

The images in climbing magazines can help you understand what *really* happens in climbing.

> **T**o be afraid of falling is natural.

## Myth #1: When a climber falls, there's nothing between her and the ground

*Reality:* Nearly all climbers use ropes and belays that keep them from falling to the ground. Falling is part of the experience of climbing. That's why we use ropes. If falling resulted in death, then we'd be reading about dozens of climbing accidents in the paper every day.

## Myth #2: Climbers are adrenaline junkies who are just cheating death

*Reality:* Like skiing, mountain biking, wind surfing, and many other sports, adrenaline rushes are part of the appeal. However, relative to the number of people participating, sports like skiing and mountain biking have more accidents and more fatal injuries than does climbing.

## Myth #3: Every year we read about a climbing accident, so it must be dangerous

*Reality:* Many of the news reports that are labeled as "climbing accidents" actually involve non-climbers (often hikers scrambling around in rocky places) who get themselves into a climbing situation. They don't have any climbing experience or any of the safety equipment that we normally use. Nevertheless, the media reports these occurrences as "climbing accidents."

## I'M AFRAID OF HEIGHTS

The fear of heights is something our mind comes up with because it knows a dangerous situation when it sees one. What your mind has not accounted for is all the safety mechanisms involved in climbing—instead, it's simply reacting without taking in the whole context. What helps is to take things slowly. You don't need to thrust yourself into a situation that causes too much anxiety; that's no fun. You need to build up a tolerance for height a little at a time. You need to assure your mind that your body is indeed safe at a particular height. To do that you may have to stop halfway up a climb and hang on the rope. Then take a look around. Climb up only as far as you feel comfortable; then stop. Once you've done this enough times, your mind will realize that there's nothing to be protected from. You may also want to do some visualization at home where you put yourself into high places and mentally experience your fear in those situations over and over again. By the time you are actually climbing and getting some distance off the ground, you will have already done it so many times in your mind that it will seem comfortable.

Carol Abel, a technical support representative in San Jose, California, says: "For as long as I can remember, I had been afraid of heights. I decided to try climbing because I'd heard that the most effective way to overcome these kinds of fears was to

> **"I** can't say I'm totally cured of my fear of heights, but it's not something I think about when I'm climbing."
>
> —Carol Abel, technical support representative

face them head-on. My first experience was at an indoor gym, which made it less intimidating. The instructor was really patient, and I was able to take it at my own pace. After a few times up the wall, I got so into the climbing part, I actually forgot about being afraid. That was three years ago, and I'm still climbing because I love it. I can't say I'm totally cured of my fear of heights, but it's not something I think about when I'm climbing."

## THE IDEA OF FALLING SCARES THE WITS OUT OF ME

To be afraid of falling is natural. Everyone experiences this fear—especially in the beginning when they're uncertain about the equipment and what will happen when they fall. I've found that if you first take some time to analyze why you're afraid, it will help you pinpoint what you need to do. If you're concerned about the safety of the equipment, the strength of the rope, the harness, or your belayer's ability to hold the fall, you may just need to have the gear and the safety techniques explained to you in more detail. If you're afraid of falling because you're worried that you might get

Relaxation and visualization can help you overcome your fears.

hurt, then you need to do a couple of things: First, watch other people fall. What happens to them? Does it appear to hurt them in any way? Second, you need to take some falls—intentionally—so that you get used to the experience of falling. Before you begin, be sure to let your belayer know that you're going to just "let go." Getting comfortable with falling can only be achieved by falling—a lot. After several falls, you'll begin to realize that it's no big deal.

Liv Sansoz is the top-ranked French climber, four-time World Cup champion, and winner of many other international titles. She says: "People are often surprised to learn that I'm afraid of falling. Recently I took a trip to the United States and made a point of forcing myself to go on lead and risk taking some falls. Initially, I was really scared, even on climbs that were very easy compared to things I've done in World Cup competition. The first few falls, I would scream and close my eyes—I didn't like it at all. But at the end of two weeks I had made a lot of progress, and I became more confident. It was one of the best things I could have done for my climbing."

## I DON'T WANT TO EMBARRASS MYSELF, SO I DON'T WANT TO CLIMB WHEN PEOPLE ARE AROUND

Being self-conscious about your performance is very common; however, it can really hold you back. You need to remember one very important thing: everyone who has ever climbed was a beginner at one time and has struggled just as you are struggling now. In fact, once you've gotten

• • • • • • • • • • • • • • • • • • • • • • • •

**E**veryone who has ever climbed was a beginner at one time and has struggled just as you are struggling now.

• • • • • • • • • • • • • • • • • • • • • • • •

past the beginner's awkward "I-don't-know-what-I'm-doing" stage, it's not over. The flailing and struggling in climbing never really ends. You may be smooth and climb with flawless technique at the level you've mastered, but each time you push your limits and try the next level of difficulty you will have a hard time. The other thing to remember is that people you will encounter at the gym or at the crag are generally focused on themselves and their own struggles in climbing; they aren't going to be paying too much attention to you.

Tiffany Keller, a schoolteacher in Sacramento, California, remembers: "The first time I went climbing it was to impress this guy I liked. I was so nervous that I was going to make a fool of myself. (I had him stop three times to use the rest room during the half-hour drive to the crag.) Finally, scratched up from the bushes we'd taken a shortcut through, and still nervous about what a klutz I was surely going to be, I started up the climb. My 'date' was giving me encouraging instructions: 'right hand up to that edge, push with the left foot.' I was so focused on what he was saying and the fact that I was getting up the route—I completely forgot all my apprehensions. Now, when I climb, the only person I'm trying to impress is myself."

## I'M TOO OLD

In the summer of 1999, 81-year-old climber Gerry Bloch made headlines for being the oldest person to climb the 3,000-foot monolith of El Capitan in Yosemite, California. I recently did some one-on-one technique clinics with a woman who I would have sworn was in her early fifties. It turns out she was 63 years old; she hadn't even *started* climbing until her late fifties! And Diane La Duca and Patricia Kelly (see chapter 1), both in their sixties, haven't let age get in the way of their passions and their goals in climbing.

According to Diane: "I was 56 and starting to notice aches and pains that took longer to go away. I began to think I was in that physical down cycle you hear about, where it's all downhill after a certain age. Around that time, I saw a much older woman than myself on the Eco-Challenge, and part of the course was rock climbing. That really inspired me, so I went out and signed up for a class. After the class I got an alert message from my body, something like . . 'Rock climbing??? I thought we were dying. . . . Yikes, I'd better get going!' And I really feel that a great body shift took place that has not only enabled me to climb, but to get stronger and healthier."

According to Patricia: "What I love about starting climbing when I was older is that nobody expects you to be any good and nobody is in competition with you, so you can just do it for yourself. The best thing is that in small increments, you do improve. I'm getting stronger. (Did you know muscles don't age?)"

Remember that climbing is a sport that rewards technique over brawn. The key to success in climbing is utilizing whatever strength you might possess in the most efficient way possible. The

● ● ● ● ● ● ● ● ● ● ● ● ● ● ● ● ● ● ● ● ● ● ● ● ● ●

"**A** great body shift took place that has not only enabled me to climb, but to get stronger and healthier."

—Diane La Duca, age 60

● ● ● ● ● ● ● ● ● ● ● ● ● ● ● ● ● ● ● ● ● ● ● ● ● ●

wise (and wisdom often comes with age) will catch on to this concept much sooner than the young and inexperienced. Remember what I mentioned earlier: if you can climb a ladder, then you can climb a rock!

### I HAVE NO ONE TO GO WITH: CAN I STILL TRY THIS?

If you don't have a partner to start out with, you have several options. No matter what, if you're a beginner you should take a course of instruction in the basics. You can either hire a guide as an instructor or take a course from a climbing gym (more on this in chapter 4). If you take a private lesson, your instructor will be your partner. If you take a group lesson, you may end up learning and practicing with another student. Once you know

Diane La Duca is proof that age doesn't matter.

the basics of safety and you're in an area that has a climbing gym, you'll find many people there—like you—who are looking for partners. Just ask someone whether they have a partner or ask two people whether they mind if you join them. You can also tell the gym staff that you are alone and looking for a partner. They check everyone in and are quite used to hooking up climbers without partners. Climbing gyms are very social environments, so don't be shy. If you don't manage to find someone, you can always go bouldering (see chapter 3), one type of climbing you can do on your own.

### THERE'S NO CLIMBING GYM IN MY AREA

Once upon a time, not so long ago, climbing gyms did not exist. And yet somehow people learned to climb. It was perhaps a bit of a journey, but if you were motivated enough, you could find a place to climb. It may take some research, such as checking with the nearest outdoor store or surfing the Web, but I guarantee there is a climbing or bouldering area somewhere in your state. Once you find an area, it may mean dedicating a weekend or at least a day to driving there. That said, you also may find a climbing wall—not necessarily a dedicated climbing gym—in your area that you didn't know was there. For example, did you know there are close to 200 YMCAs in the United States that have climbing walls? You'll find more ideas in chapter 4 (see also chapter 10, Resources).

A women's-only class may be offered at a local climbing gym.

## I'M PREGNANT: CAN I STILL CLIMB?

From what I've heard, there are few sports that you can begin after you become pregnant that you didn't participate in before you were pregnant. For example, if you're a runner before you become pregnant, then you can run well into your pregnancy. The same goes for climbing. If you are already a climber, you can climb while pregnant. Alison Osius, an editor at *Climbing* magazine, was still climbing in the eighth month of both her pregnancies. Alison says, "I climbed during both pregnancies, up until two weeks from delivery. I could still climb (after a fashion) then, but I started to feel the harness press on my sides a bit while lowering, so I stopped. I heard people had been whispering, 'Should she be doing that?' But I was talking about it with my midwife the whole time. And I had two healthy, 8-pound babies."

Obviously there are some limitations and precautions that you'll need to take if you choose to climb while pregnant. You should only climb on top rope, because you don't want to risk taking falls on lead. You may also need to buy a different harness—possibly a full-body harness if you climb late into your pregnancy. Be aware that your balance and strength, relative to your increased weight, are dramatically different. Many women have found climbing to be frustrating in the later stages of pregnancy, when the size of their bellies make it difficult to see their feet and they have a hard time finding their balance.

# Chapter 3

# TYPES OF CLIMBING AND TYPES OF CLIMBERS

I t's time to delve more deeply into this sport called climbing. Within the sport there are several disciplines and styles of climbing. Some climbers participate in all of them, while others practice just one. Many times, as was the case with me, a climber will spend chunks of time specializing in one type of climbing and then will move on to another. Usually a need for a greater challenge, or simply a *different* challenge, precipitates the shift. After reading this chapter, don't expect to know which type of climbing will suit your style. This is simply an overview and a way for you to get familiar with some new words you'll be encountering once you get started. Once you have the basic skills, you will be able to try them all if you like and discover which one(s) you enjoy most.

All of the climbing described below, with the exception of bouldering (covered later in this chapter), requires a partner. When you are climbing, your partner will belay you (using a safety system involving rope and a friction device), and when it's her turn to climb, you'll be the belayer. Belaying is the most crucial element in the safety system, and it will be covered in greater detail in the following chapter.

It's impossible to describe the different types of climbing without using some technical words. Along with the term *belayer*, I mention several other techniques that you may not understand straight away. Bear with me and know that all of this will make more sense as you progress

## CHOOSING TO BE A TOP-ROPE-ONLY CLIMBER

• • • • • • • • • • • • • • •

Like a lot of women, Kathy began climbing on top rope. She loves the movement of climbing, how fit and light she stays, and the social aspects of being at the crag with her friends. She's tried leading several times, but mentally she just turns to jelly because she's terrified of falling. Although she realizes that leading could be mentally more satisfying, she simply doesn't have any fun climbing on lead. In the last year or so, Kathy decided to stop torturing herself and now she climbs only on top rope. She says, "I wish there wasn't such a stigma about top roping. Because of my huge fear of falling, I find that dealing with leading routes is almost more than I can bear. I love to climb, and on top rope I can concentrate on the moves without the terror! My climbing has improved since I've accepted the fact that I may not be a good lead climber."

through this book. I've also chosen to use the climber's terminology (and sometimes slang words) in some instances, and I follow these words and phrases with more common terminology in parenthesis. You might as well start learning now what you'll be hearing once you get started.

### TOP ROPE CLIMBING

Almost everyone begins climbing on *top rope* because it's the safest and least intimidating way to start. The term *top rope* comes from the way the rope is rigged from the top of the climb. In top rope climbing, the climber is tied into one end of the rope, which runs up to an anchor point and then back down to the ground where the *belayer* (the person who will hold the climber's fall) has the climber on *belay* (the safety mechanism that helps the belayer arrest a fall). As the climber ascends, the belayer takes in the *slack* (the loop of rope) that is created with the climber's progress. Because the rope is always above the climber, if the top roped climber falls no real "falling" occurs. The climber simply sags onto the rope and is held in place by the belayer until she's ready to pull back onto the climb or be lowered.

Another way to top rope is to *second* or *follow* a climb. The terms *seconding* and *following* are synonymous; they mean that someone else led (see the following section entitled Lead Climbing) the climb, and the climber is now climbing it while being belayed by the leader from above. This method is used most commonly in traditional climbing, which is also described below. Although the actual climbing moves you do on top rope are essentially the same as what you would do on lead, many people consider an

On **top rope**, the climber always has the rope above her so there's little risk of falling any distance.

ascent of a route on top rope to be less of an accomplishment than doing the same route on lead. The reason for this is simply that there is no risk of falling any distance when on top rope, whereas on lead, the climber must execute the same moves, but with the added mental challenge of knowing that she may take a fall while trying to do them.

## LEAD CLIMBING

For most climbers, as they develop the basic skills of safety and movement and become more comfortable with climbing on top rope, the next logical step is to learn to lead climb. *Lead climbing* requires more mental involvement and commitment than having a top rope always above you, which minimizes or eliminates falling altogether. In lead climbing, the leading climber is tied into her harness with one end of the rope, which is trailed along as she climbs. The trailing rope goes down to the belayer, who is *paying* (feeding) out rope through a belay device. The climber periodically clips the rope into a *carabiner* that is attached to a piece of *pro* (protection or gear). If the leading climber falls, the belayer will stop the fall with the help of the belay device, which creates friction and takes most of the force of the fall. The falling climber

When **climbing on lead**, the climber trails the rope behind her and clips it into protection points as she ascends.

### TAKING THE LEAD
• • • • • • • • • • • • • • • • • •

Sonya and her husband got into climbing together. They started by driving on weekends from their home in Portland, Oregon, to Smith Rocks, Oregon. Initially, Sonya's husband learned to lead from the guide who had been their instructor. Sonya was content to follow. It wasn't until Sonya took a weekend trip with a less-experienced girlfriend she had met at the gym that she was forced to get on the sharp end of the rope (that is, to lead the climb rather than do it on top rope). Comments Sonya, "I couldn't believe how much more intense my awareness was, how much more focused my mind was. Suddenly, a whole new world opened up for me—even though I'd been climbing steadily for a year. Now, after two years of climbing on lead, I feel very solid. I realize that I actually climb better and more precisely with that slight bit of tension that is created when I know I *could* fall. That's why I really prefer to lead. And mentally, it's so rewarding to push yourself beyond your fears, to keep your head together when you're on the thin line between falling and staying on."

## BOULDERING: AN EASY WAY TO GET YOUR CLIMBING FIX
• • • • • • • • • • • • • • • • • • • • • • • • • • • • • • • • • • • • • • • • • • • • • • • • • • • • • • • • • • • •

Deb, a single mom, finds that bouldering is the most efficient and logical use of her time. With soccer games and gymnastics on the weekends, if it weren't for getting to the gym to boulder a couple of times a week, some weeks she wouldn't get any climbing in at all. When her children get out of school in the afternoon, Deb takes her two daughters, ages 5 and 7, with her to the gym. According to Deb, "The girls love climbing but they're too young to belay, so we all just boulder around the gym. The floors are padded and the maximum height they're allowed to go is marked, so I don't worry about them falling off." Deb has also met a few friends who have invited her to go bouldering outside while the girls are in school. "Bouldering is very physically demanding, so in two or three hours, everyone is pretty spent. I can get a great workout and be back in time to pick up the girls," she says. Deb recently entered a local bouldering competition at the gym and took third in the intermediate category; she can't wait for the next competition.

Bouldering with a partner spotting.

falls onto her last piece of protection, as the rope is locked off by her belayer. Because the climber's rope is never above her, she is at risk of falling double the distance she is *out* (away) from her last point of protection.

If a climber takes a lead fall, she can actually drop some distance, whereas a fall on top rope, with the rope above her, results in no dropping—she's simply hanging on the end of the rope. Lead climbing is the more satisfying of the two types, but it is also more committing because of the potential for real falls.

### BOULDERING

*Bouldering*—climbing on boulders or at the bases of cliffs with just climbing shoes and a chalk bag (a small bag containing chalk used to prevent sweaty hands)—may be the simplest of all climbing pursuits. The climber doesn't climb very high off the ground, so there is no need for a rope or a belay. Usually the bouldering climber can jump or fall off the boulder without injury. Strictly speaking, *boulder problems* refer to designated sequences of relatively few movements—say 3 to 10 moves. Because there are fewer moves to a boulder problem, the individual moves that a climber can pull off are generally more powerful than what she could do on a long route. However, many people boulder by doing long traversing-style climbs, close to the ground, where they may or may not follow a designated sequence.

Depending on the features of the rock or the artificial wall, the climber can make the problems as hard or as easy as she wants. Bouldering has become extremely popular recently; there are many people who *only* boulder and never tie into a rope. The great thing about bouldering, especially indoors, is that it allows a climber to experiment with new types of movement and to get stronger physically. If she gets in trouble, she can simply step down to the ground. In a gym, the possibility of hand and footholds is tremendous. Most gyms have a specific bouldering area and also allow you to climb on any of the walls without a rope, as long as you stay beneath their designated "bouldering height," usually 10 to 12 feet off the ground. It's great to boulder with at least one other person so that you can spot each other when jumping or falling off problems. However, bouldering can be done alone and is a way to go climbing when you can't find a partner to belay you.

## SPORT CLIMBING

Along with bouldering, sport climbing is one of the fastest growing segments of rock climbing. Because of the relative safety of sport climbing, climbers can push the limits of their physical abilities. *Sport climbing* is like any climbing that requires a rope and a belay, but sport climbs are *bolted*

(they use preplaced, permanent protection points that have been drilled into the rock), so the leading climber doesn't have to place her own protection. She need only carry *quickdraws* (sewn webbing with carabiners at either end) to clip into the eye of the bolts as she climbs; it's much faster and easier than having to place her own removable protection.

Because sport climbers don't spend as much effort placing pro, the difficulty of the individual moves they can do is greater. And because they have more confidence in the safety of bolts, sport climbers take more falls than *trad* (traditional) climbers do. Sport climbing also requires less of a time commitment, because sport climbs by definition are usually fairly short routes—no more than half a rope's length. Usually the climber is lowered to the ground from permanent anchor bolts at the end of the route. The sport climber rarely climbs to the top of the cliff. Gym or indoor climbing on artificial walls also falls into the category of sport climbing.

Climber attempting a difficult, overhanging **sport climb**.

# THE APPEAL OF SPORT CLIMBING

Since learning to climb nine years ago, Karen has tried almost all types of climbing: bouldering, trad climbing, even big wall climbing. (*Big wall climbing* is used to ascend long routes on very tall cliffs or walls. Most of the time these ascents require a multiday effort due to the length of the route, and the climbers often use their gear to make upward progress.) In the past several years, she's spent more time sport climbing than she has doing any other type of climbing. Karen has always made it a priority to live near a major climbing area, and she recently landed a job in Denver. With a new and very demanding career, she finds that her time is limited. On the weekends, Karen mainly goes to a sport climbing area called Rifle on the western slope of the Rockies. Like many sport crags, there is a high concentration of climbs in a fairly small area, so she can get a lot of routes in. She says, "The challenges with each type of climbing are different. When I was into bouldering it was mastering explosive moves. In trad climbing it's mastering the gear and learning to set up safe anchors. But the thing that I really love about climbing is the movement. With sport climbing it's all about the movement. You can work out the moves on a climb until you find the right body positions; this allows you to do moves you thought were incredibly hard the first time you tried them."

Hanging out on top after climbing a multi-pitch trad route. Note the typical **trad climbing rack** in the foreground.

## TRADITIONAL CLIMBING

*Traditional* or *trad* climbing emphasizes the use of *removable protection* (also called *natural protection*) placed by the leading climber. A trad climb can be a *single-pitch* (one rope length) or *multi-pitch* (several rope lengths) climb. The leading climber places her own protection, or pro, as she ascends the route. The pro a trad climber uses includes such items as spring-loaded *camming* devices and various wedge-shaped metal blobs on wire cable called *stoppers* or *nuts*. These devices are inserted into cracks and constrictions and are attached to the climber's rope by a carabiner. The *seconding climber* (the climber following the pitch on top rope) will remove the pro. Because these devices take some effort to place correctly, most climbers cannot do moves that are as powerful or sustained as what they could do on a sport climb. The challenge in trad climbing, however, isn't purely physical; there are the added psychological elements of calculating how often to place pro, dealing with pushing

A **camming device** has a trigger that retracts when pulled, narrowing the width of the cams so the device can be inserted into a crack. When the trigger is released, the cams expand to fit the crack. They push against the walls of the crack, forming an unmovable anchor to stop any downward pull, such as by a falling climber.

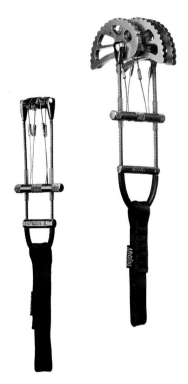

on when you can't find a placement, and trusting that the pro you've placed will hold a fall.

Many of the earliest developed climbing areas were trad climbing areas because the natural *lines* (usually cracks) were the most obvious weaknesses to climb. Once all the crack lines had been established—that is, climbed for the first time, named, and graded—the climbers of that era then climbed the *faces* between the crack climbs. *Face climbs* are routes that are often protected by a combination of bolts, which have been left in the rock where the rock is *blank* (without any natural features), and natural protection, wherever it is possible. Face climbs can also be protected entirely with bolts; however, there are usually far fewer bolts on these climbs than on modern sport climbs because of the era in which they were established.

## ROCK AND ITS INFLUENCE ON TYPES OF CLIMBING

The type of rock influences, if not dictates, what type of climbing you'll do. Many traditional climbing areas were established in the 1960s and 1970s. They are on lower angle cliffs that have many prominent features. What attracted the first climbers were the weaknesses of these areas, such as cracks that allowed the climbers to (1) ascend the route using the crack with their hands and feet jammed in it (a technique known as *jamming*), and (2) place removable gear to protect them in case of a fall. For these reasons, you'll find that most traditional climbs are crack climbs.

Granite, basalt, and sandstone are three types of rock that often have crack formations, and climbing areas with these types of rock are often established trad climbing areas. Classic examples include Yosemite, California (granite), the Canyonlands in Utah (sandstone), the Gunks, New York (granite), and the Tennessee Wall near Chattanooga, Tennessee (sandstone).

Sport climbing routes are bolt-protected face climbs often on vertical or overhanging rock that is very featured. The features, such as edges, *pockets* (holes), *scoops* (a hollowed-out, concave impression on a rock face), knobs, grooves, *ribs* (thin, convex shapes that can be pinches), and *dimples* (small, round depressions), are what the climber uses with her hands and feet. However, these sport climbing routes are face climbs, so they don't accept removable protection the way cracks do. Certain types of rock—such as limestone, sandstone, and some types of volcanic rock—tend to be more featured. The advantages of climbing routes on very featured rock are the many options and combinations of moves that can be done. Examples of well-known sport climbing areas are Smith Rocks, Oregon (volcanic), Rifle, Colorado (limestone), and the Red River Gorge, Kentucky (sandstone).

# WHAT'S A CLIMBING AREA?

The term *climbing area* refers to the site of a cliff or crag where there are established climbing routes. A climbing area may have just one cliff or it may refer to a region with several crags; the different crags within the climbing area will also be named. For example, the climbing area called the Red River Gorge in Kentucky encompasses several different crags within the several-mile radius of the region. Torrent Falls, The Mother Lode, Roadside, Military Wall, and Left Flank are among some of the crags that collectively make up the climbing area called the Red River Gorge. A climbing area is usually named for the city, town, state or national park, or geographical location near which it's located.

There will almost always be a guidebook for an established climbing area, which can usually be found in outdoor stores in the region. You can often find guidebooks for many of the well-known, destination climbing areas, such as Yosemite and the Canyonlands (Utah), in shops all over the country. Guidebooks to climbing areas are a great source of information on the nature of the climbing, what gear you'll need, regional weather, camping or lodging options, recommended routes, park fees, local guide services, and driving directions, as well as basic topographic maps of the crags themselves.

Here is a short list of some of the better-known climbing areas in the United States and Canada. See the sidebar beginning on page 160 for other climbing destinations.

| | | |
|---|---|---|
| Squamish, British Columbia | Rifle, Colorado | The Gunks, New York |
| Joshua Tree, California | City of Rocks, Idaho | Smith Rocks, Oregon |
| Yosemite, California | Red River Gorge, Kentucky | Canyonlands, Utah |
| Eldorado Canyon, Colorado | Red Rocks, Nevada | New River Gorge, West Virginia |

Many small-to-medium-sized crags are scattered throughout City of Rocks National Reserve in Idaho.

## FREE CLIMBING VERSUS FREE SOLOING

The term *free climbing* is almost always confused in the minds of the nonclimbing public with the term *free soloing*. Like many climbers, I have been asked countless times, "Do you do that free climbing stuff?" It's usually asked with wonder and fear because the intended question is, "Do you free solo?"

In *free soloing*, the climber makes upward progress with her hands and feet on the natural features of the rock (just as in *free climbing*), but she uses no equipment, such as ropes and other gear, to protect her in the case of a fall. If the soloing climber falls, there is nothing to prevent her from falling to the ground; serious injury or death is the result. As you can imagine, not many people are keen to take these kinds of risks. In fact, only a handful of climbers in the world free solo. However, because the mainstream media prefer sensational stories, free soloing has gotten more attention than the type of climbing that most of us do, which is, of course, *free climbing*. With the common word "free" in both terms, you can see why people get the two terms mixed up. This confusion of terminology exists only in the nonclimbing public. Just as climbers use the term *climbing* instead of *free climbing*, we also use the term *soloing*, rather than *free soloing*.

You may enjoy climbing on some types of rock more than on others. I can't tell you what the "best" type of rock to climb on is because it's different for everyone. Climbing preferences are like any personal preference. I might think Thai food is the best food in the world but for you it's Italian; neither of us is right (or wrong), it's just that we each have our own opinion about what's best. However, I can say that you'll probably most enjoy the type of rock that you can climb well on; this is just human nature. Certain types of rock have features that are more natural or more intuitive to climb on. And certain types of climbing may also seem easier than other types. For example, you may find that you naturally climb easily on face climbs, especially those that aren't very steep. Usually areas with low-angle face climbs (also called *slabs*) are easier for beginners. This type of climbing is more straightforward, and using the holds is more obvious. Crack climbing, on the other hand, is a learned technique and not at all intuitive. Learning to crack climb can be frustrating and exhausting for the beginner. Once learned, however, it can be super fun.

### MORPHOLOGIC CLIMBING

There are some types of rock that can be harder (or easier) to climb, depending on your size. I describe climbs such as these as being *morphologic*; however, this is my own climbing lexicon and you won't hear many other climbers use this term. (I borrowed the word from the French *morphologique*; French climbers *do* use this term to describe size-dependent climbs.) An example of morphologic climbs would be crack climbs. In crack climbing, the size of the crack will favor some climbers' hand or digit sizes, while it will be more difficult for others who don't fit as well. For example, in a crack that is very thin, a woman with smaller fingers could more readily get her fingers into the crack than could a man with large fingers. Some crack climbing routes will be harder for a woman than the grade indicates, while others will be very easy for the grade (see next page). This is because the majority of routes were originally climbed by men and subsequently graded by men, so the grading reflects the difficulty for the typical man-sized hand or fingers.

Other types of morphologic climbing are height-dependent routes. Typically, women are shorter than men; on certain types of rock, a shorter height can make the climbing more difficult. Sandstone is often the worst offender in this case—especially on face climbs. At some sandstone crags, the routes often have big blank sections between fairly good holds. With absolutely no other features between the holds, a short climber may not be able to do certain moves—or if she can do the move, it's a lot more difficult. You may hear people refer to routes like these as being *reachy*. Quite often, taller people do not realize a route is going to be a lot harder for a shorter person because they themselves didn't have any trouble with it. Be aware that even easy-graded climbs can be quite difficult on rock without many intermediate holds, such as sandstone. As with crack climbing, the routes were probably graded for the average-size guy. Climbing areas like this can be tough, if not downright frustrating, for someone short. Examples of areas that have size-dependent or morphologic routes include Eldorado Canyon, Colorado, and the New River Gorge, West Virginia. In both of these areas, the rock is sandstone.

## WHERE DOES INDOOR CLIMBING FIT IN?

Artificial climbing walls do a decent job of mimicking the movement of most face climbing you would find outside. However, climbing only on plastic (as it's commonly referred to) won't allow you to develop certain movement skills necessary for real rock. Artificial holds are easier to see

because they're usually brightly colored shapes bolted onto a wall. Real rock, on the other hand, is usually more subtle, and it's harder to read the moves because the holds are part of the natural shape of the stone. This is particularly true when using your feet. On plastic, the footholds are quite big and stick out from the wall: easy to see, easy to use. Outside on natural rock, the holds just aren't that evident. Only climbing outside can teach you the art of finding holds and the more subtle techniques of using them.

Indoor climbing is a great way to familiarize yourself with the movement of climbing and the safety techniques so that when you do go outside, you can focus completely on the experience.

**Artificial climbing holds** are more obvious and easy to figure out how to use than holds on natural rock.

## CONFUSING TERMS: AID CLIMBING VERSUS FREE CLIMBING

Once upon a time—and still today on big blank expanses of rock—climbers used any means necessary to ascend a climb. That meant sometimes using their equipment—such as ropes and hardware—to make upward progress. This is usually done by clipping a ladderlike webbing foot loop called an *étrier* into the protection points and then standing in one of the foot loops to reach up to make the next placement of protection. However, in the 1960s, climbers began to "free" climb climbs that had previously been ascended with the "aid" of equipment. *Free climbing*, as it came to be known, simply means climbing a route "free from the use of aid" (the opposite of *aid climbing*). Instead, the free climber uses only the natural features and irregularities of the rock with her hands and feet to make upward progress. As in aid climbing, the free climber uses ropes and places gear (protection points), but this is only a backup in case she falls. The gear is not used to ascend, as it is in aid climbing. Today's climbers almost never use the term *free climbing*; trad climbing, sport climbing and bouldering—all technically *free climbing*—are referred to simply as *climbing*. The term *free climbing* is, however, specifically used in reference to an aid route (one not previously free climbed) that is finally ascended free, as in "Lynn Hill is the first person to *free climb* the Nose."

That said, plastic is incredibly fun to climb on for the same reason. The holds are easy to see and easy to figure out how to use. For a beginner, this is a real plus. Indoor climbing is a great way to familiarize yourself with the movement of climbing and the safety techniques so that when you do go outside, you can focus completely on the experience.

### THE RATING SYSTEM

In climbing, the path we take up a climb is called a *route*. Routes are named and given a grade of difficulty (called a *rating*) by the first climber to climb the route. The rating system is a fairly subjective way to describe a route's difficulty relative to other routes in that area. How easy or how difficult a route is rated depends on many factors: how steep the route is, how big the holds are or what size the crack is, how long the route is, how continuously difficult it is, and how easily it can be protected. The rating system is not perfect, but it can give you an indication of the level and intensity to expect before you start up the route. The grades of routes are often the source of much talk and debate among climbers.

Artificial holds.

The way people ascend in the mountains is divided into classes. *First class* is defined simply as walking along a trail. *Second class* is hiking up steep inclines. *Third class* includes use of both the hands and the feet over rocky terrain. *Fourth class* involves climbing on fairly easy but steep and exposed terrain, where a fall could result in serious injury. *Fifth class* is technical rock climbing, in which the use of ropes and belaying is required. In North America, the difficulty of a route is rated using a grading scale called the Yosemite decimal system: all of the ratings begin with a "5" (for fifth class) followed by a decimal point and a number that describes how hard the route is. The ratings begin at 5.0 (easiest) and go up to 5.14 (hardest), but the scale is open-ended. Thus, the top end can expand as the difficulty standards in climbing are pushed.

**Rating Scale**

5.10a

5.10b

5.10c

5.10d

5.11a

5.11b

5.11c

5.11d

and so on

Somewhat confusing at first is the rating scale after 5.9. From 5.10 through the end of the scale (currently 5.14), the increments are no longer simply 5 plus a whole number. They are broken down further into a, b, c, and d, so the ratings are as shown above.

The incremental difference in difficulty between a route rated 5.11a and a route rated 5.11b is the same as the difference between 5.8 and 5.9. We're stuck with this odd rating scale because when the system first started, it was believed that nothing harder than 5.9 could be climbed, which made it a closed system. When the climbers of the day finally (begrudgingly) added 5.10, the rating encompassed a wide range of difficulty of routes. Later on, climbers finally realized the folly of this and decided that the routes that were rated 5.10 needed to be broken down further to reflect the *real* differences in difficulty. So today, the next rating to be added to the scale will be in increments of a, b, c, and d, before it goes to the next higher number.

For ranking the difficulty of boulder problems, North American climbers use V grades. This, too, is an open-ended system with V plus a number, beginning at V1 (easiest) and going up to V14 (hardest). The grade of a boulder problem is determined by how hard the moves are and how difficult it is to execute all the moves in one push. Typically, the bouldering climber must work on a boulder problem before they're able to do it. The moves in a given problem are fairly difficult relative to those found on roped climbs, but the climber can readily and repeatedly try the moves; falling is fairly safe because you're so close to the ground.

# Chapter 4

# GETTING STARTED

It is essential that you find someone to teach you the basic safety and movement techniques of climbing. While this book can teach you a lot about climbing by providing in-depth descriptions, drawings, and photographs, it is still just a book. You cannot learn the actual physical mechanics of safety from any book; it requires hands-on experience with an instructor to show you how the ropes, the hardware, and the specialized techniques are used to safeguard the climber. Because there is some inherent risk to this sport, you cannot go out climbing and hope to figure it out on your own. Climbing is not a sport that lends itself to a trial-and-error approach.

For the safest and most productive learning experience, I highly recommend getting professional instruction. Even if you know an experienced climber who is willing to introduce you to the sport, you still may want to opt for a professional. Rebecca Rusch, veteran climber, gym owner, and instructor both indoors and out, says, "Most people assume that their friends who climb will suffice as qualified guides. This is a costly assumption for a couple reasons. First, you have no guarantee that your friends are practicing impeccable safety procedures. It may seem safe to you, but as a beginner you do not have the qualifications to double-check your friends. Secondly, a good climber is not necessarily a good teacher. Your climbing friend may be able to climb safely and with great technique, but communicating these nuances to a student in a clear

• • • • • • • • • • • • • • • • • • • • • • • • • • •

"**A**lthough instruction may be expensive, it's a sound investment in your safety and future enjoyment of this new sport. It's also a great way to meet new partners who share your new interest."

—Rebecca Rusch, veteran climber and instructor

• • • • • • • • • • • • • • • • • • • • • • • • • • •

way is an entirely different skill. Although instruction may be expensive, it's a sound investment in your safety and future enjoyment of this new sport. It's also a great way to meet new partners who share your new interest."

## WHERE TO GO

Before we get into how to find an instructor or course, you'll need to consider what type of learning environment would be right for you. When I began climbing so many years ago, the only place to climb was on natural rock cliffs. Today things are much different. The cliffs and crags still exist, but indoor walls and climbing gyms have cropped up in nearly every major city (and quite a few minor ones) across the United States. Today's would-be climber can learn most skills indoors, go outside for the "real thing," or do a combination of both. The experience of climbing can be quite different depending on the setting. For this reason, in the rest of this chapter and elsewhere in this book, I separate the information for indoor climbing and outdoor climbing. To help you determine what will be the best option for your first experience, I include what you can expect from each venue and then distill this into a list of the pros and cons of each.

### Climbing gyms

*Climbing gyms* are facilities that are meant to replicate rock cliffs; their walls are made of fiberglass, sand, and resin panels or of textured plywood and are covered with artificial holds (also made of a fiberglass-sand-resin mixture). Climbing gyms are a place to practice rock climbing where weather and time of day have no effect. The environment is relatively safe, very accessible, and not too intimidating.

In the last several years climbing gyms have become the primary locations for beginners trying out the sport. Instructors are available for basic instruction whenever the gym is open, and you can rent the gear you'll need—such as a harness and shoes—until you're ready to get your own. The cost of instruction varies depending on the part of the country, but a basic introductory class ranges between $25 and $40, which includes a day pass so you can climb on your own after the lesson. Because most beginners do not own their own gear, nearly all of the gyms include a harness, shoes, and a belay device in that price. If you already have your own gear, the cost of your first lesson could be $5 to $8 less. For instruction past the basic safety stuff, most gyms offer both private and group lessons. One-on-one instruction is the most expensive, so if cost is an issue you may want to get a couple of your friends in on the lesson. Many gyms also offer regularly scheduled group clinics for those looking to improve some aspect of their climbing. These types of classes usually require that you sign up in advance, and some also require a deposit.

Amanda Tabor of Stamford, Connecticut, talks about indoor gyms: "I learned to climb at an indoor gym mainly because the nearest crag was two hours away. It wasn't until I'd been climbing for six months that I finally went to a real crag. Wow, what a difference! I'd felt so in control in the gym, so protected. That first time outside made me feel very exposed. It took going a few more times before I really felt confident outside. I didn't know it would be so different. I have to admit, I'm glad I started out indoors."

As with just about anything else, climbing gyms have both pros and cons.

## Pros

- **Convenience.** If you live in a city with a gym, travel is minimal.

- **Controlled learning atmosphere.** No extra stresses, such as exposure or extreme height, are involved. The floors are soft, and the area is relatively small and comfortable.

- **Customizable instruction.** Many different options of angles and holds are available, so the instruction can be tailored to your needs.

- **Minimal time commitment.** With such a compact area, you can learn the basics and get climbing in as little as one to two hours.

- **Ease of communication.** You and the instructor are never a great distance from each other, so the instructor can easily give advice while you're climbing.

- **Cost.** Instruction in the basics is relatively inexpensive compared to going outside (see Cons section below for additional cost considerations).

- **Time and temperature control.** It doesn't matter what time of day or night it is or what the weather is.

- **Social atmosphere.** This is a great place to meet new climbing partners or to find a belayer.

## Cons

- **People.** The popularity of climbing means that you may be dealing with crowds at certain times of day or in periods of bad weather.

- **Ambience.** A climbing gym lacks the "wind in your hair" experience of being outside.

- **Limitations for learning certain types of climbing.** You can't learn crack climbing, placing gear or setting *anchors* (multiple protection points at the top of a route to secure the belay position), rappelling, or the judgment skills needed for traditional climbing.

- **Cost.** While the basic course may be inexpensive, you'll pay for a day pass or membership with each subsequent visit.

## Climbing outside

The advantage of climbing outside is that it's *the real thing*; you'll climb on real rock, not simulated rock. Also, many climbing crags are located in really beautiful places. Your experience will include hiking to the climb, the scenery along the way, and the feeling of being in nature. You'll learn the subtleties and texture of climbing on natural rock, as well as the thrill of getting to the top of that piece of rock and the views you'll have from that point. The exposure of being up high can be tremendously exciting. However, if you're the less adventurous type or are afraid of heights, that exposure could be intimidating.

Denise Ketterman of Walnut Creek, California, recalls her first climbing experience—outdoors—in only positive terms: "My first time climbing was absolutely magical. I was so amazed at things like the texture of the granite, the features of the rock, and how cool it was to have climbed to the top of this pinnacle. There was nothing above me but sky, and I could see for miles. I now climb indoors a bit, especially during the work week, but it's only to stay fit for my real passion—cragging!"

Travel time is a consideration if you're climbing outside because most crags are, at the very least, outside the city limits, and more often, they're some hours' distance away by car. With the drive, the hike in and out (there aren't too many crags right next to a parking area or highway), and the lesson, you will likely spend most of a day. If you go to a trad climbing area, you'll learn about the gear, anchors, and general safety in multi-pitch climbing. However, when you're actually climbing, it may be difficult to hear your instructor if she is belaying you from above. Unlike indoor climbing with its variety of holds and angles, what you learn could be limited to the style of climbing that area offers. Also, learning to climb outside will almost always be more expensive than learning at a gym.

As with climbing gyms, climbing outside has its pros and cons.

# Pros

- **Atmosphere.** You'll be outside, in nature, in a scenic environment.

- **Realism.** You'll experience real rock, real exposure, real climbing.

- **Greater learning opportunities.** If you are multi-pitch or trad climbing, you will be learning more about how to be safe in those situations.

- **Fuller experience.** Your experience will include hiking, carrying your gear on your back, climbing to the top of something, and the overall experience will be more of an adventure.

- **Fewer people.** Usually you won't have to deal with crowds, although there are some areas (such as Yosemite National Park) that are wildly popular.

## Cons

- **Greater time commitment and less climbing.** With driving time, hiking time, and the distance between climbs, the actual time you have to climb will be less than going to a gym.

- **Cost.** With the greater responsibility and time commitment on the part of the instructor, the price of learning outdoors can be more than triple the cost of learning in a climbing gym.

- **Limitations for learning certain types of climbing.** You'll learn only the style of climbing that type of rock offers.

- **Weather and time restrictions.** Your trip could be cancelled or cut short due to bad weather and because your climb must fit into the daylight hours.

- **More exposure.** The experience can be fairly intimidating for the first-time climber depending on tolerance for heights and exposure.

- **Communication.** On multi-pitch climbs, it can be difficult to hear your instructor when you're climbing and the instructor is belaying you from above.

### IF YOU DECIDE TO LEARN INDOORS

If there's a gym in your area, it should be pretty easy to find. Here are some tips for locating a place to climb indoors.

### Dedicated climbing gyms

If you have a choice, a gym dedicated to climbing is your best option for learning indoors. Dedicated climbing gyms have more walls and more terrain changes and angles, and they are more focused on serving their climbing customers. Nearly all of them offer both roped climbing (lead and top roping) and bouldering. If there is more than one gym in your area, you may want to see all of them to get an idea of what each offers before making a decision. As a beginner, you will find features like the friendliness of the staff and the overall atmosphere more important than the overhanging terrain of the walls or the price of admission.

The resources chapter (chapter 10) contains an extensive list of indoor gyms. If you don't see one in your city, don't give up the search because this list is not complete, and new gyms are opening all the time. There may also be a wall in a health club or other location not dedicated specifically to climbing.

The best place I've found to get information about climbing (indoors or out) is a local climbing shop—check in the yellow pages under sporting goods. If you can't tell from the listing, call the general sporting goods stores to find out whether they have a climbing department. If so,

**T**he best place I've found to get information about climbing (indoors and out) is a local climbing shop.

speak to someone there who is knowledgeable about climbing; if there's a local gym, that person will know about it. Many climbing gyms and shops are also listed in the classified advertising pages of climbing magazines as well as on many World Wide Web sites.

## YMCAs, health clubs, and other fitness facilities

Because climbing has gotten (and is still getting) a lot of attention as a more fun and mentally challenging way to get a workout, more and more mainstream fitness gyms are building climbing walls in their facilities. About 200 YMCA facilities have climbing walls. The Sporting Club (an upscale health club chain with locations in major cities, such as Atlanta, Chicago, and Los Angeles), Chelsea Piers in New York City, and several World Gyms across the United States all have climbing walls. Many university recreation centers have climbing walls as well, although these are sometimes available only to students, staff, and alumni. Some of these locations charge a rate that allows you to use all of their facilities, and some have cheaper rates if you'll only be using the climbing wall. The costs vary depending on the going rate in your region of the country. Your best bet is to look in the phone book and place some calls before setting out.

## What to expect from your first indoor climbing lesson

Most gyms take beginners on a walk-in basis; however, you should call ahead and make sure that you don't need to schedule an appointment for instruction. You'll also want to verify the price of the basic lesson and whether that price includes gear rental.

When you arrive, your sign-in procedure will take longer than any other time you'll climb there. You will be presented with a waiver, which you'll be asked to read and initial in several sections as well as sign at the bottom. For obvious liability reasons, the gym will not let anyone climb without having a waiver on file.

## What to bring and what to wear

The clothes you wear should allow freedom of movement without being too loose or baggy. Wear the kinds of clothes you'd wear to work out in at an athletic club. Fabrics like cotton Lycra jersey are great; it's stretchy, comfortable, and not too bulky. Jeans are out because they have no stretch. The same goes for your khaki shorts or any pants or shorts with a zipper or button fly. Pull-on pants or shorts with elastic waistbands are best. T-shirts, tank tops, sports bras, bike shorts, and sweatshirts are all acceptable. Even though the climate is controlled, I always bring a sweatshirt or microfleece jacket in case I get cool when I'm not climbing. If you think it could be hot, bring a sports bra and shorts. The best clothing for climbing I've found is clothing that is designed specifically for the movement of climbing and wearing a harness. I've listed a few of the companies that make climbing-specific clothing in the resources section.

For the rental climbing shoes you'll be wearing, you may want to bring a pair of socks. Bring the thinnest pair you can find. Most climbers don't normally wear socks with climbing shoes, but for the sake of hygiene, you may not want to put your bare feet into shoes that dozens of other people before you have worn. It won't really affect how you climb, especially your first few times.

Besides your clothes, you may also want to bring a water bottle. The gym will have a drinking fountain, but it's nice to have plenty of water close at hand. Although climbing is not aerobic, you can definitely get dehydrated. It's important to drink a lot of water.

Stretchy, comfortable clothing that allows freedom of movement is what to wear for climbing, whether you're climbing indoors or out.

## Facilities

The facilities vary wildly from gym to gym; however, at the very least you can expect a women's changing room with lockers and at least one shower. Most of the gyms don't have locks for the lockers, so bring your own if you need to secure your personal items or, better yet, leave your valuables at home or in your car. If you intend to shower at the gym, you may need to bring your own towel. Call ahead to find out what the gym provides.

## Rental gear

The gym will outfit you with a harness, climbing shoes, a belay device with a locking carabiner, and possibly a chalk bag. The rental gear you wear—the harness and the shoes—will serve you better if they fit right.

## Harness

The *harness* is the device you'll wear that secures you to the rope. It consists of a waist belt and leg loops constructed of nylon webbing. The webbing may or may not be padded—an unpadded harness is less comfortable but no less safe. You'll hold the harness up by the waist belt with the leg loops oriented just as they would be on your body; then you'll step into the harness as you would a pair of pants. Most people need a little help with this part the first time, so don't feel self-conscious about not being able to figure out which end is up. The gym staff will help you adjust the waist belt and leg loops and will make sure that the buckle on the waist belt is doubled back. *Doubling back* the buckle is the most critical safety step in putting on a harness (see chapter 7 for a more detailed explanation of this process). If doubling back is not explained to you, you may

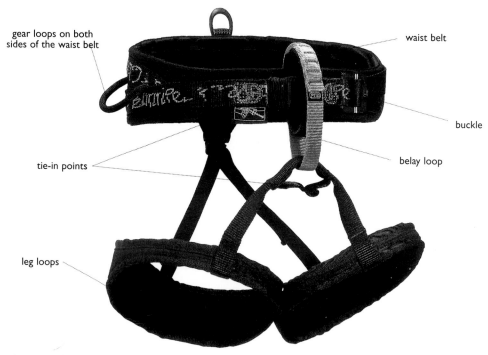

gear loops on both
sides of the waist belt

waist belt

buckle

tie-in points

belay loop

leg loops

Climbing harness.

want to ask the person helping you to show you how to do it. If the leg loops are adjustable, fit them so you can fit your hand between your thigh and the webbing.

Here are some guidelines to help you determine whether the harness fits:

- The waist belt should be snug, but not tight, at the smallest part of your waist.

- The harness should not feel as if it's pulling down onto your hips or as if the leg loops are going up your bum. If it does, it's too short in the rise.

- Nothing should feel too tight or binding. If it does, ask whether the harness can be adjusted or whether they have another harness style or size you can try.

## Shoes

Your rental shoes either will have laces (like a normal running shoe) or will be the type you can slip on, which are called *slippers*. The staff person from the gym will probably ask you your shoe size and then take an educated guess at your size. Climbing shoe sizes are not the same as street shoe sizes, and they aren't consistent among brands. Use whatever size the staff person determines is correct and go from there. However, don't hesitate to ask whether they have more than one model of shoe available in your size, so you can get the best fit possible.

Fit is the trickiest part. The shoe should fit pretty snuggly, with your toes right at the end of the shoe. If the shoes are too big or roomy on your foot, they'll impede your progress. As a beginner, you may not be able to stand the pain of properly tight shoes yet, and it won't really matter for your first few times. However, try to avoid a floppy fit. Remember that you can unlace the shoes or even take them off when you're not climbing.

At this point, you'll have your harness and shoes on and you will have probably been given a belay device attached to a locking carabiner. You're now ready to begin learning the language of climbing safety, how to use the belay device and other safety procedures, and ultimately the basics of movement. Because climbing is a sport of some risk, the instructor will start by teaching the rituals of safety and how the gear is used and then go on to the movement.

## Climbing signals

The climber is dependent on the belayer for her safety when she falls and when she is being lowered from the climb. Climbing signals are used between the climber and the belayer so that there is a clear understanding of what's happening, especially as it pertains to the belay. This verbal exchange is a ritual that is intended to help avoid accidents. Here is what you will learn to say, even before you learn how to belay or climb.

- **"On belay?"** The climber asks this as a question. She is asking the belayer, "Am I *on belay?*" This means, is it safe for me to begin climbing? When the climber is on belay, the ropes, the belay device, and the carabiner are connected properly and are in the ready position; see "Belaying the climber" below.

- **"Belay on."** If the belayer has the climber on belay, then she would respond to the climber by saying, "*belay on,*" which lets the climber know that she can begin climbing.

- **"Climbing."** The climber announces this to the belayer just before she leaves the ground.

In actual practice, many gym climbers neglect to use all of these signals. Often the belayer just says "belay on" and the rest is verified visually because the climber and belayer are standing next to each other. However, to pass the gym's belay test so that you can climb and belay on your own, you will be required to demonstrate that you know the proper signals.

## Belaying the climber

You will learn how to belay before you even learn how to physically climb. Belaying is as much a part of the sport of climbing as is the movement of climbing itself. Although climbing is thought of as an individualist sport, for safety reasons you will have a climbing partner. While you're climbing, your partner will be your belayer. Once you have climbed and are back to the ground, it will be your turn to be the belayer while your partner climbs.

Here's how belaying works. The belayer uses a friction device called the *belay device*, which is attached to her harness, and she feeds rope through this device. In the event that the climber falls, the friction created by the belay device coupled with a firm grip on the rope with the belayer's *brake hand* will arrest the fall. Don't worry that you won't be able to hold the fall with your brake hand; the belay device actually does most of the work of stopping the fall.

In the case of a fall, the safety of the climber rests in the hands (literally) of the belayer, which means your greatest responsibility in climbing is when you are the belayer. That's why this step of the lesson is the one your instructor will be testing you on before you are allowed to belay on your own. But first the instructor will take you step by step through the procedure of belaying; you'll have an opportunity to hold someone's body weight to get the feel of it, and you will run through the belayer's duties one by one, with plenty of practice, before you are allowed to climb.

As a beginner, you will first be learning how to belay someone who is climbing on top rope. You won't learn how to belay someone lead climbing until you've mastered this first step. What follows is a step-by-step description of a top rope belay lesson.

1. **Rigging the belay device.** The way you thread the rope into the device will vary based on the type of belay device you're given to use. The four most common devices for belaying are the *Grigri, tubular-type, sticht-type,* and *figure 8* devices (see Belay Device, pages 127–28).

   Because each device is different, I can't give many generalizations about how to rig the rope. This is definitely a hands-on situation. The only way to learn how to rig the device is to have your instructor walk you through it. After you've seen it done by the instructor, you should try it on your own a couple of times until you get it.

2. **Attaching the device to your harness.** Regardless of what belay device you use, once it's threaded it must be attached to the *belay loop* on your harness with a locking carabiner. Be sure to have the instructor indicate clearly which part of the harness is the belay loop (see illustration page 48). Once the carabiner is attached to the belay loop, lock the locking mechanism on the carabiner. There are many different locking mechanisms available on carabiners, so again I can't give you much guidance here. This is a hands-on learning experience. Remember this step is extremely important and always deserves a double check.

3. **Feeding rope into and out of the device.** Once the device is rigged and attached to your harness, you will be shown how to pay out rope and how to take in rope through the belay device—all the while keeping one hand (the brake hand) on the rope. It will be stressed in no uncertain terms that your brake hand cannot come off the rope at any time. This is the part that can be tricky because it requires some getting accustomed to. Don't be surprised if at first you find that keeping your brake hand on the rope while feeding and taking in the rope seems

terribly awkward or even impossible to do. With practice, you'll get the hang of it and you'll even become smooth and coordinated with the movements. Mastering this skill is critical because it is the essence of safe belaying and safe climbing.

In this first lesson, you'll probably be doing more taking in than paying out of the rope because that's the motion you'll use when belaying someone on top rope.

4. **Holding someone's fall.** Before you actually belay someone from the ground to the top of a climb, the instructor will probably have you feel the sensation of holding a fall. Remember that a climber on top rope will have the rope above her, so she doesn't really take falls of any distance. What you will be holding is her body weight as she sags onto the rope. You will—or should—have the opportunity to belay someone who climbs up a short distance and then lets go on purpose. The person—the instructor or another student—will only get high enough off the ground so you can experience the sensation of holding her fall.

Just before the person takes that practice fall, you'll probably be a bit nervous. Even though the instructor will tell you (and I'm also telling you) that it's not that hard to hold someone's fall, it's not until you actually do it that you'll feel confident that you can. At that point, you will realize how little effort it takes to hold someone and that it is truly the belay device that does most of the work.

5. **Belaying the top roped climber as she climbs up.** In top roping, the rope will be running up from the climber, through the fixed anchors, and back down to the ground where it will run through the belay device, which is attached your harness. After you've communicated to the climber that the belay is on and it's safe to climb (remember the signals), the climber will begin ascending the route. As the climber ascends, there will be excess rope (a loop of slack) created by her progress. It's your job as the belayer to *take in* that slack through the belay device. The belayer taking in rope should pace herself to match the rate of the climber's ascent. This way the climber never has too much slack nor is kept too tight with the rope. If the climber should fall, her weight would come onto the rope and the belayer would hold her with the aid of the belay device and the brake hand.

6. **Lowering the climber.** In top rope belaying, your last responsibility will be to get the climber back down to the ground safely. You'll usually need to do this when the climber gets to the top of the climb. To learn to lower someone, you will probably practice this technique on either the instructor or another student. Again, the best way to practice this is by trying it when the climber isn't very high off the ground. This way, if you make a mistake, nothing too tragic can occur.

To lower the climber, you will take the climber's weight just as you did with the practice fall. You'll hold the climber in place for a moment, simply to reassure

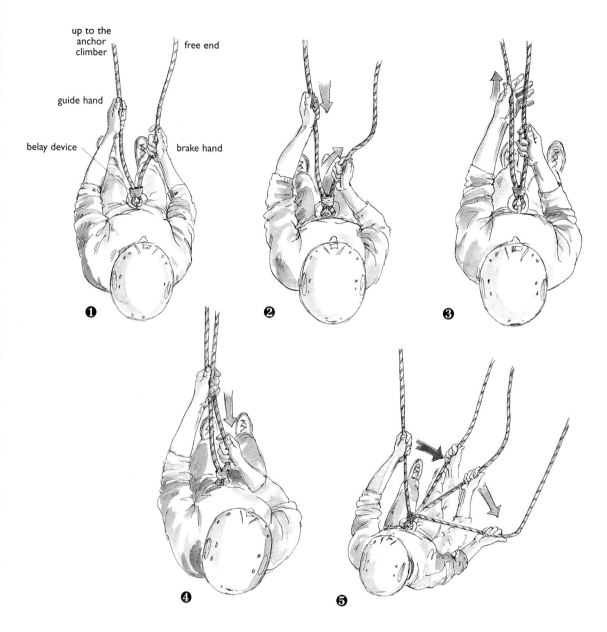

**Top rope belaying.** To belay a climber on top rope, the belayer is primarily occupied by taking in the slack rope that is created when the climber ascends. Once the rope is rigged through the belay device and is attached to the harness at the belay loop, the belayer grabs each end of the rope with a hand. The belayer's **guide hand** holds the rope that goes up to the anchor point and back to the climber while her **brake hand** holds the free end of the rope (**1**). Both hands must remain on the rope for all the procedures of taking in the slack. As the climber progresses, the belayer's hands work in concert: her guide hand pulls the excess of slack rope into the belay device while her brake hand pulls that rope out of the belay device (**2**). Before the belayer can take more rope in with her guide hand, she must slide it back out along the rope (**3**), then grab both pieces of the rope just above the brake hand (**4**). Once her guide hand holds both sides of the rope tightly, her brake hand is free to slide back down toward the belay device in preparation to pull more out from the device. To arrest a fall, the belayer pulls her brake hand off to the side, bending the rope across the belaying device (**5**). The two strands of the rope coming from the device should be at an angle of 90 degress or even a bit more.

her that you have control of the belay. Then, slowly at first, you will begin letting the rope slide back through the belay device. You will control the rate of rope going back through the device with your brake hand. The instructor will guide you through the actual mechanics of lowering with the particular device you're using. Watch the climber as you are lowering her to make sure she's descending at a smooth, gentle rate.

7.   **Passing the belay test.** To be allowed to climb on your own, you will be required to put all of the skills above to the test. Once you pass this test, you will get a card or some other means of verification that says you know how to belay. Because you will be responsible for another person's safety, the gym has to take this precaution.

Don't worry about passing the test the first time around. You can always take it again. Simply try to relax and do your best. Your instructor will probably be the one that oversees your belay test, so think of it as just another practice part of the lesson. Remember: the gym wants you to pass this test too, so you will come back and give them money to climb there.

## Your turn to climb

The next step is learning how to tie into the rope, how to physically climb, and what to do when you're the one being lowered. You may have been given a *chalk bag*; now is the time to put it on. Usually this small bag of gymnast's chalk (carbonate of magnesium) has some sort of waist belt or cord so you can hang it from your waist, just above the top of the harness waist belt. Chalk is not an essential safety item; however, some climbers consider it an absolute necessity for preventing sweaty hands. You will probably forget to use it your first few times climbing. As you progress to harder routes with smaller handholds or if you find yourself slipping off holds because your hands are too sweaty, you will find chalk to be wonderfully useful.

## THE BELAY LOOP

Something even your instructor could be mistaken about . . .

Most harnesses these days have both a separate *tie-in point* (where the rope is threaded to secure the climber to the end of the rope) and *belay loop* (where the belay device is attached with a locking carabiner). However, there is quite a bit of misinformation about the belay loop. Some climbers and even some instructors don't use the belay loop because they mistakenly believe the tie-in point is safer for belaying. This is an erroneous belief and, in fact, belaying from the tie-in point could put pressure across the gate portion of the carabiner (known as *cross loading*), with the potential for breaking it. *No* harness or carabiner manufacturer recommends belaying from any point except the belay loop. The belay loop is the single strongest part of the harness, and its breaking strength is greater than nearly all carabiners.

## SAFETY RITUALS

• • • • • • • • • • • • • • • • • • • • • • • • • • • • • • • • • • • • • • • • • • • • • • • • • • • • • • • • •

Contrary to popular belief and the media hype, climbers are actually very safety conscious. There are many rituals of safety that we practice to ensure that we have long and healthy lives. You'll find we do a lot of checking and double-checking. In the beginning, you might feel that some of these safety practices are being hammered into your brain repeatedly. This is because the cause of accidents in climbing is almost never due to failure of equipment. Rather, climbing accidents are usually due to human error; it is the weak link in our system. And so, we have pinpointed the most common human errors and have made a practice of emphasizing the importance of *not* making these same mistakes.

I've ranted in this chapter about double-checking your safety systems. You will hear this from your instructor as well. As a beginner, you should get in the habit of double-checking three things: the buckle on your harness (see note below), the knot you've tied in with, and the locking carabiner to ensure that it is in the locked position for belaying. To help you do this *every* time, I offer a suggestion that works for me. Each time you climb or belay, create a cue to do these checks. Your cue could be either a physical action or a verbal one. For example, the moment you've finished lacing your shoes, you double-check your knot and your buckle. Or your verbal cue could be to ask yourself aloud, "Am I doubled back? Is my knot tied?" This is my personal favorite because it makes me pay attention and answer the question. Sometimes I simply ask my climbing partner those questions, so both of us are checking the system. Whatever your cue, it should trigger a little safety ritual: to look down and check whether your buckle is doubled back, your knot is followed through, or your locking carabiner is locked.

Don't hesitate to check your partner's equipment, too. Asking your partner whether she has checked her knot or whether her harness is doubled back is something even experienced climbers do with each other. It's always appreciated. Don't worry about sounding like a safety nut—in climbing, that's a virtue and nothing to be ashamed of. I guarantee that nobody will ever make fun of you for it.

**Note:** Petzl harnesses have a patented DoubleBack buckle. If you have one of those harnesses, the waist belt always remains in the doubled-back and safe position, so you need only worry about the knot and the carabiner.

## Tying into the rope

*Tying into the rope* is another important safety practice. You tie directly into your harness rather than using a carabiner to clip into the rope. The fewer links in the chain, the better.

Before teaching you the knot you'll tie in with, your instructor should show you how make sure both sides of the top rope are hanging free and clear. Most gyms require you to use a followed-through figure 8 knot to tie into the harness. This knot is the only knot that gyms allow because it's fairly easy to master, it doesn't readily work itself untied, and you can usually judge whether it's tied correctly by looking at the shape of the knot. If everyone in the gym is tied in with a figure 8, the staff has a much easier time verifying that their customers are tied in correctly.

With the end of the rope in hand, your instructor should walk you through the steps of tying this knot. The first part of the knot you tie should have the figure 8 about 3½ feet from the end of the rope. This 3½-foot end is called the *tail*. You'll take the tail and thread it through the tie-in

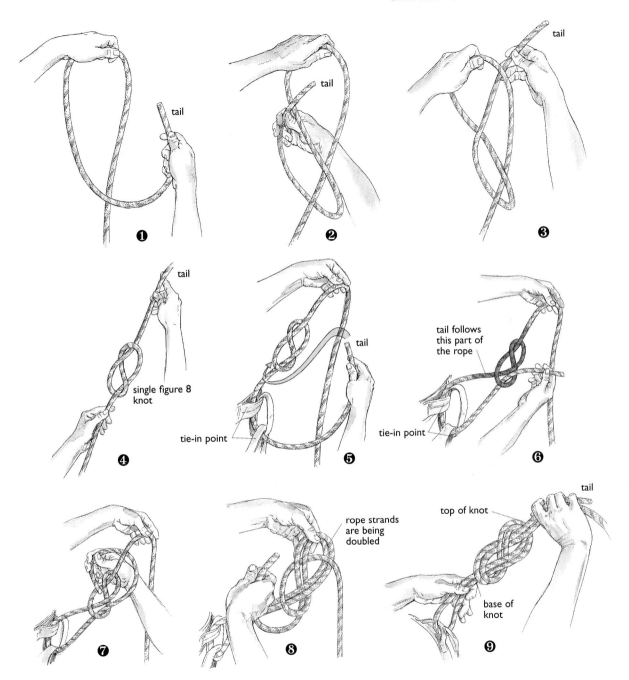

The knot that attaches the rope to your harness is known as a **tie-in knot**, the most common is the **figure 8 follow-through knot**, shown here. **1.** Make a loop about 3½–4 feet from one end of the rope. **2.** Wrap the tail around the loop you're holding and thread it into the front side of the loop. **3.** Pull the tail through to form the **single figure 8 knot**. **4.** The resulting knot will have approximately 3 feet of tail coming out from the top. **5.** Thread the tail through the **tie-in point** of the harness, bringing the knot a few inches from your harness. **6.** Begin threading the tail back into the single figure 8 knot by following or tracing the shape of the single figure 8 with the tail now coming out from your tie-in point. **7.** Continue following the shape of the knot, creating the same figure 8 knot with the tail. **8.** The last follow-through step brings the tail out of the top of the knot. **9.** Correctly tied figure 8 follow-through knot: the base of the knot is 3–4 inches away from the tie-in point and the tail coming out of the top is at least 6 inches long.

point on your harness. Your instructor will show you where the tie-in point is on the harness (see illustration page 48) you're wearing. However, be aware that not all harnesses will have a tie-in point like the one you're wearing at the time.

Once you have the tail threaded with the knot pretty close to the harness, you will take the tail and follow it through the figure 8 to complete the knot. Once you've finished this *follow-through* step, you should end up with a tail of rope sticking out of the completed knot that is at least 6 inches long. This step is the most critical; a knot that has not been completely followed through is not safe. This is one of those steps that requires double and triple checks. Even very experienced climbers check their knots and those of their partners—you should too.

## Climbing

Once you're tied in and you have a belay, you can start climbing. Your instructor will probably already have you tied into a rope that's on an easy climb—something graded in the 5.5 to 5.7 range. The instructor will be the best judge of what routes in the gym are good for beginners, so climb what she recommends. Pay attention to the grades of the routes you're climbing so you can start to understand the rating system.

For the physical movement of climbing, please refer to chapter 5, where I give you an edge over the average beginner by going beyond what you'll learn in the typical basic lesson. In the basic lesson, you'll be given only the bare bones version of climbing movement. However, I firmly believe that having the knowledge and awareness of what good technique is—even if it's gained just from reading this book—can make a huge difference in your first experience. These techniques, learned at the beginning, will be the key to all of your future success in climbing.

Climber in the correct body position for being lowered (the correct position is the same whether you're climbing inside or outside).

### Being lowered

Before you read chapter 5, I cover one last topic that relates to climbing: getting back down. You learned earlier in this chapter that you would be lowering the climber back to the ground with the belay device. When *you* get to the top of the climb, it will be your belayer's job to lower you. Sounds a lot easier, doesn't it? Actually, it's not. Not initially. Many people have a hard time putting their life in someone's hands. That sounds a bit extreme, but the feeling, that first time, of leaning back on the rope and trusting that your belayer is going to get you safely back down to earth can be very disconcerting. As the climber being lowered, you have no control of the belay and the rate of descent. I promise you, the first time you're lowered is the worst time.

After that first time, once you realize that there is nothing to worry about, you'll wonder what all the fuss was about.

Here's what you'll need to know about being lowered to make the experience easier and more pleasant. The moment you put your weight on the rope, you will need to lean back and straighten your legs. Think about being seated in a chair but with your legs straight out in front of you.

Keep your legs perpendicular to the wall and "walk" your feet down the wall as you descend. You may need to keep telling yourself to lean back in order to keep the correct body position. When your belayer begins lowering you, you may instinctively react by grabbing the rope and leaning toward the wall with your body or bending your legs. Avoid this reaction; otherwise, your legs and knees will drag against the wall and you may even smack your face on the wall in front of you.

## IF YOU DECIDE TO LEARN OUTSIDE

While indoor climbing is convenient and has many other pluses, nearly all climbers agree that the reason we climb indoors is to train and practice for doing the real thing outside. And few would disagree that climbing on real rock is more fun than is climbing indoors. Certainly, as you will see, there's a lot more to the experience when learning outdoors.

Here are some sources for finding an instructor or guide for climbing outside.

### Guide services

Guide services are typically based near or at climbing areas. Their clients learn their skills on real rock. With most guide services, you can take a private lesson (more expensive) or a group lesson (less expensive). On average, you can expect to spend between $90 and $150 for private instruction; for group courses, the fee ranges from $35 to $75. Even if you don't have any friends to go with, ask the guide service whether they offer a regular schedule of group courses. You may also want to find out whether they offer women-only courses. If they don't already, they may be willing to put something together for you.

The more established guide services will either include gear in their fee or have you rent it separately. Locally, your best resource for finding a guide service will be to inquire at an outdoors store. Often, these stores let the nearest guide schools stock their brochures in the store. Also ask to speak with someone in the climbing department (preferably a climber) and ask this person for a recommendation, because there may be several guide services to choose from. If you have access to the Internet, there are many climbing web sites with links to guide services all over North America, as well as to some in foreign lands.

Keep in mind, as with any business or individual, there are good guide services and there are not-so-good ones. A guide service

> While indoor climbing is convenient and has many other pluses, nearly all climbers agree that the reason we climb indoors is to train and practice for doing the real thing outside.

that is AMGA (*American Mountain Guides Association*) *accredited* has passed certain criteria for the structure of their business (including a brief review of their climbing activities, hiring policies, permits, and insurance).

Be aware, however, that accreditation is simply a general review, not an in-depth evaluation of the company's guides or their skills. An individual guide can be AMGA *certified*, which means the guide has passed some rigorous testing of actual climbing and guiding abilities, client care skills, and emergency and risk evaluation skills. However, not all guides working for AMGA-accredited guide services are themselves AMGA-certified guides.

I wouldn't necessarily say that you should go *only* with an AMGA-accredited guide service or that you should insist on an AMGA-certified guide, because I know of several excellent guide services and guides that are *not* accredited or certified. In fact, some guide services that were formerly AMGA accredited have disassociated themselves from the AMGA because of political or philosophical differences in the structure of that organization. If you do find a guide service that's not AMGA certified, don't rule them out; they could be great. Once you've received an independent recommendation of a guide service, here are the important questions to ask before making a decision:

1.    Does the guide or guide service have insurance?

2.    Can the guide or guide service give you a list of previous clients for references?

3.    How long has the guide service been in business? How long has your guide been guiding?

4.    Has the guide had any accidents? If so, what happened?

5.    What type of emergency medical training does the guide have?

6.    What skill level and training does the guide service require of its guides?

## Other outdoor guides and instructors

In many parts of the country, some outdoors stores and indoor climbing gyms have climbing schools that take courses outside. These courses are usually run as a separate business, and so they should be investigated the same way you would a guide service.

## University outdoors programs

Many universities have teaching and guiding programs for outdoor, nonteam sports such as rock climbing. The cost is usually fairly reasonable because they are catering to students. Most of the instructors in these programs are other students. Because of limited budgets with these programs, the level of instruction is pretty basic. However, for entry-level learning, this is a good and fairly inexpensive way to go. They may or may not have gear to rent, depending on how well funded their program is. The major drawback is that their classes may be available only to students and staff.

## Climbing clubs and associations

Some cities have local climbing clubs that run trips and offer classes. These organizations are not for profit, and their members are local climbing enthusiasts but not necessarily experts. The courses tend to be inexpensive (or even free) but also sometimes infrequent. The excursions they offer are usually to outdoor climbing areas. While the trips they run may be inexpensive, I am hesitant to recommend this as your first climbing experience because there is no guarantee of the quality or expertise you may encounter. If you find a club in your region, try to make some inquiries at a climbing shop or gym about the group's level of expertise.

## Women-only courses

There are also a few guide services that offer "women-only" seminars or workshops for all levels. These group trips are not frequent, every-weekend occurrences. In fact, depending on which one you choose, these workshops may only be offered two to four times per year. To take part, you'll need to do some planning. The big advantage of a women-only course is the very supportive atmosphere, in which the learning is structured *for* women and the skills are taught *by* women.

Women That Rock—founded and still organized by Mattie Sheafor, a long-time mountain guide for Exum Mountain Guides in Jackson Hole, Wyoming—is one of the better known of this type of seminar (see the sidebar for more information). There are also guide services that specialize in women's programs, including First Ascent. Based near Smith Rocks, a world-class crag near Bend, Oregon, First Ascent has at least four women-only trips a year in Oregon, California, and Nevada because First Ascent co-owner Carol Simpson believes "this type of format is the most supportive and fun way for women to learn and progress in climbing." She elaborates: "It's not just that the women are learning skills and

**T**he big advantage of a women-only course is the very supportive atmosphere, in which the learning is structured *for* women and the skills are taught *by* women.

### WOMEN THAT ROCK

Now in its tenth season, Women That Rock is one of the most highly acclaimed and popular outdoor programs in the nation. Originally based in Jackson Hole, Wyoming, the group now offers extended workshops in the Sierras of Northern California and the Red Rocks of southern Nevada in addition to a one-day event in their original location in Grand Teton National Park in Jackson Hole. Women That Rock offers a positive learning environment because of its small, professionally guided sections that provide great student-to-teacher ratios. The instructors are some of the most accomplished women climbers in the United States and are chosen for their abilities as teachers and mentors, not just for their abilities as climbers.

The costs for the courses range from $130 to $490. All profits go to the following charities: Access Fund, the American Alpine Club, and the Nation's Missing Children Organization and Center for Missing Adults.

For more information, see Women That Rock and Exum Mountain Guides in chapter 10.

. . . . . . . . . . . . . . . . . . . . . . . . . .

"It's amazingly empowering to find out that you're not alone, that what you're experiencing is normal and OK."

—Carol Simpson, climbing guide

. . . . . . . . . . . . . . . . . . . . . . . . . .

techniques from a female instructor; they're often learning that the other women in the class are experiencing the same fears, the same insecurities, the same frustrations. It's amazingly empowering to find out that you're not alone, that what you're experiencing is normal and OK."

## Adventure travel

There are a huge number of adventure travel companies out there now that offer all kinds of "adventure sports" trips—including climbing. Do your homework first and find out who runs the climbing trips they offer. Usually these outfits are working with different guide services for each sport discipline. It may be that they are using an independent guide or guide service in the area you're interested in. In that case, check their rates and find out whether you'd be better off working directly with the guide service or whether the package includes things you'd be interested in, such as lodging or even airfare if the trip is to a destination climbing area. No matter what, you still need to check all references and ask about liability insurance.

## What to expect from your first outdoor climbing lesson

Once you've decided which guide service or course to take and you've reserved a date, you'll want to find out what they expect you to bring and what they provide. Be sure to ask whether the climbing gear (harness, shoes, belay device, locking carabiner, and helmet) is included in the price of instruction or whether there is a separate charge to rent them. Usually, the service will have a checklist that they can mail or fax to you. They may even want you to sign and send back a waiver before the day of your class. Besides the climbing gear, the usual gear that you should bring for a day of climbing includes the following:

- **Clothing.** See the details listed below.

- **A full water bottle.** Carry at least a liter.

- **Packable food.** Include such items as trail mix, apples, oranges, and health bars.

- **Appropriate walking shoes or hiking boots.** Find out what the approach is like to determine how beefy your shoes need to be.

- **Sunscreen, bug spray, toilet paper, and lip balm.** You will need bug spray most in the eastern part of the country. The rest of the items are necessary for being out all day in the sun.

- **A day pack or backpack.** You'll be carrying your own stuff as well as the climbing gear you'll rent, so make sure your pack is big enough.

## Clothing

For your clothes, always think "freedom of movement" without too much bulk or bagginess. Nonstretching fabrics, such as denim, twill, and chino, aren't ideal. Wear the kinds of clothes I recommended earlier in this chapter for indoor climbing—stuff you'd wear to an athletic club for a workout. One exception to this would be the type of leotards worn in dance or aerobic classes. When you're climbing outside and nature calls, you may find the only place to relieve yourself is behind a bush with very skimpy leaf coverage. That's when you'll wish you weren't wearing a leotard.

Before you head out, be sure to look at the weather forecast. Bring plenty of warm clothes if the weather is going to be cool or windy. I usually bring a jacket or sweatshirt, even if the forecast calls for good weather. Climbing areas are typically at higher altitudes or in the mountains, and weather can change fast there. Also, once the sun goes down or the cliff comes into the shade, it can get chilly despite the warm temperatures the weather forecast predicted for the nearest city.

## Rental gear

You will either be renting the harness, shoes, and helmet directly from the guide service or be directed to a climbing store or gym that rents gear. Whatever the case, follow the fit guidelines I describe earlier in this chapter for indoor climbing gear rental. With the exception of the helmet, which is not used in indoor climbing facilities, the rest is the same.

You'll need a helmet for climbing outside because of the possibility of *rock fall* (or other things dropped from above, such as gear and water bottles) and in the rare case of falling upside down and hitting your head. As a beginner climbing on top rope, the latter possibility is almost nonexistent. However, even though it's rare at most established climbing areas, rock does fall and people above have been known to drop things accidentally. The helmet that you use must be a climbing helmet; you cannot use a helmet from another sport because even those that look like climbing helmets have not been tested for the kinds of impact encountered in climbing.

## THE CALL OF THE WILD (AND NATURE)

One thing few instructors will teach you is how to pee while wearing a climbing harness. For years I would take my entire harness off, but that's not really possible on a multi-pitch route unless there is some big ledge where you're in no danger of falling off. I finally was shown by a fellow climber (thank you, Bobbi Bensman!) how to pee without taking off my harness. The straps that hold the leg loops up in back are very elastic, so the leg loops can quite easily be pulled down when you pull your pants down. You have to pull them down only to about mid-thigh for them to be sufficiently out of the way, and there's plenty of stretch in the elastic for that. This system also saves a lot of time because you don't have to take the harness off and then put it back on. There are now some harnesses that have a *drop seat* option, which allows you to unclip the leg loops in the back. In this situation, the waist belt can remain on; you simply have to be careful to get the leg loops and straps out of the way before you start to pee. If you do opt for taking your harness off, be sure that you remember to double back the buckle on the waist belt when you put it back on.

• • • • • • • • • • • • • • • • • • • • • • • • • • •

For all the gear you rent, make sure you're pleased with the fit and comfort before you head out. Once you reach your destination, you will be stuck with your choices.

• • • • • • • • • • • • • • • • • • • • • • • • • • •

Proper comfort and fit of the helmet will make your first climbing experience more enjoyable. However, you probably won't have a lot of choice when it comes to rental helmets. Most guide schools will have one type of rental helmet available. Some outfits buy the cheapest helmet on the market, which aren't likely to be the most comfortable or adjustable. When you try the helmet on, ask for assistance in adjusting it to the correct position on your head. If offered a choice, ask what the guides wear. Because they're wearing their helmets all the time, they probably own the most comfortable model available.

For all the gear you rent, make sure you're pleased with the fit and comfort before you head out. Once you reach your destination, you will be stuck with your choices.

Before you set out, make sure all of your rental gear and your personal gear fits in a pack that you can wear for the hike.

## The learning environment

As I mentioned earlier, you'll have to hike some distance (called the *approach*) to get to the climbing area itself. Once there, you'll begin learning the same sorts of things I described in the indoor lesson. Everything from putting your harness on to lowering a climber is identical whether you are indoors or out. So if you skipped ahead to this section, back up and read that previous section. The information that follows here is what you'll learn *in addition* to what is taught at an indoor gym.

It is impossible to describe every situation that you may encounter outside, because there are many different scenarios that could take place depending on the climbing area you're visiting. Some of the factors that determine what you'll do include the height of the cliff, the length of the route, and whether the instructor can walk to the top of the crag to set up a top rope or whether you will be belaying her as she climbs and then sets the top rope. What I describe here are the most common first-time experiences; however, your lesson may vary from that shown here depending on where you learn.

## Climbing signals

The signals you learn for indoor climbing are an abbreviated adaptation of a system that was created for the outdoor climbing environment. Climbing signals are really a code language that was developed as a basic, concise way for the belayer and the climber to communicate—especially when the climber is out of sight or far from the belayer. By using a few short words consistently, a climber that is out of sight of her belayer can call out a certain single word and be assured that her belayer has understood. Most of these signals are used in traditional climbing, especially on multi-pitch climbs. Please read the signals ("on belay?" "belay on," and "climbing") that I've already described in the indoor lesson above, because those are common to both venues. If you are top rope climbing with your instructor on the ground, these three signals may be all you need. If you are multi-pitch climbing, however, these are the other calls you'll learn:

- **"Off belay."** When the climber has secured herself into the *anchor*, she calls down to the belayer so that the belayer can take the climber *off belay*. This allows the climber to freely pull up the rest of the rope until it is taut to the belayer, who will become the seconding climber.

- **"Belay off."** Once the belayer hears the signal that her climber is safely tied into the anchor, she will *de-rig* (unlock the carabiner and remove the rope from) her belay device and call up to the climber to indicate that the rope is now free to be pulled up.

- **"That's me."** This is a call that is used only when the leader is belaying the seconding climber from above, as in multi-pitch climbing. Once the leader has set the anchor, she begins to pull up the remaining rope that she didn't use on the pitch. The seconding climber is tied into the other end; once all of the slack has been pulled up and the rope is taut to her harness, she will call up "That's me" to let the leader (soon to be her belayer) know that all of the excess rope is up. At that point, the belayer will put the seconding climber on belay.

- **"Up rope."** This phrase is spoken by the seconding or top roped climber to the belayer to request that the slack in the rope be taken up. This usually happens if the belayer cannot see the climber and is unaware that the climber has progressed upward, creating a loop of slack rope above the climber. The climber may have slack rope from time to time during the climb, but she will use the phrase "up rope" when the slack rope coincides with a feeling that she may fall.

- **"Slack."** This is usually spoken by the leading climber to the belayer to indicate that she needs extra rope to be fed out so she can clip into a piece of protection or the anchor. Occasionally, it will be used by the seconding or top roped climber to indicate that she needs some rope to be fed out so she can *down climb* (climb down by reversing moves to get to a lower position on a climb) or *traverse* (climb sideways rather than straight up) or to indicate that the belayer is keeping the rope too tight.

- **"Rope!"** This is shouted down before throwing a rope down from the top of a cliff when setting up a top rope, setting up a rappel, or pulling a rope down after a *rappel* (a descent on a rope using a friction device). This alerts anyone below that there is a rope about to come down. A 200-foot rope thrown even

## THE IMPORTANCE OF SIGNALS OUTSIDE

• • • • • • • • • • • • • • • • • • •

Many gyms don't mention the use of all of the traditional climbing signals because the climber and the belayer are never very far from each other. The indoor instructors will usually teach you to indicate when the belayer has the climber on belay by saying, "belay on." However, you may not learn much more than this. Many climbers in gyms who didn't learn the traditional signals use vague terminology—such as "OK" or "you're on"—to let the climber know that she's on belay. This is fine for the indoor environment; however, if you plan to also climb outside, especially on multi-pitch climbs, you should familiarize yourself with the climbing signals in this chapter. Shouting "OK" to your belayer or your climber could be too ambiguous because there isn't a common understanding of what that means.

half its length can create a tremendous whipping momentum and can injure if it smacks someone at the end of its flight.

• **"Rock!"** This is shouted down anytime there is a falling object to alert anyone below of the danger. Of course, it's appropriate to call out "Rock!" when there is a rock falling, but the same term is used for all falling objects. This is the simplest way to communicate the urgency and importance because a water bottle, or even a very small object such as a carabiner, hurtling into someone at terminal velocity can cause serious injury or even death.

• **"Watch me."** The climber says this when she wants the belayer to really pay attention. This is usually said if the climber is about to make a move where she feels she could fall. It's like saying, "I'm not certain I can pull this off, so be aware—I could fall here."

• **"Falling!"** If the climber knows she's about to fall off the climb, she should warn the belayer. This helps the belayer be ready to hold the fall. Of course, the climber may not always know when she's about to fall, so it is up to the belayer to be diligent in her belaying.

### Signals for the sport climber

There are some signals more specific to sport climbing that you should know. These terms are less universally known—and it's less critical that they be known—because the climber and the belayer are never a great distance from each other. Most of the signals in sport climbing have to do with making the belayer aware that something other than climbing is taking place. Like all of the signals, it's important to use these terms to make your climbing safer.

• **"Take."** In sport climbing, *take* is often used instead of *falling*. This tells the belayer to lock off the belay device and hold the climber at that point of the climb, if she is on top rope, or to be prepared for a leader fall, if the climber is on lead. The climber uses *take* because typically she wants the belayer to also take in any slack in the rope to make the fall shorter and to keep the climber at a certain spot on the climb. *To be taken* means to be held by the rope. This term replaces *falling* to warn the belayer that the climber is coming off.

- **"Straight in"** or **"Safe."** When a climber connects herself directly into the anchor with webbing and carabiners that are attached to her harness, so she can safely untie the rope from her harness, she is said to be *straight in*. This expression is used in sport climbing by the climber to let the belayer know that the climber is *straight into the anchor* and will be pulling up slack so that she can thread the anchor before being lowered. This signal does not mean off belay—here the climber is indicating only that she is temporarily not in need of an active belay. Once the anchor is threaded, the climber will need to be *taken* by the belayer and lowered to the ground.

- **"Back on you"** or **"Take me."** The climber says this once she has threaded the anchor and wants the belayer to *take* her so she can detach herself from being *straight into* the anchor and can then be lowered to the ground by the belayer.

## Learning to belay

All of the climbing you'll be doing when you learn will be top roped. However, there are two types of belaying that you could learn. The most common type is when you are belaying in a top rope situation, which is precisely the same as that described earlier for indoor climbing. Depending on the area you go to, you may need to learn how to belay a leading climber, which would be your guide. You would only need to learn this if you climb a multi-pitch route, or you climb at a single-pitch crag where the guide cannot walk to the top of the crag to set up the top rope. These situations are less common because guide services and schools have found areas where it is quick and easy to set up top ropes without having to climb a route and rely on the belay of an inexperienced climber.

## Lead belaying to set up a single-pitch top rope

There are times when it isn't possible to walk to the top of the cliff to set up a top rope. Your guide or instructor may have to lead the climb to set up the top rope. You will be taught to rig the belay device and make certain the locking carabiner is locked, just as you would for top rope belaying. Your instructor may tie you into some sort of anchor point (a tree, pro placed in a crack at the base of the route, and so on) so that you wouldn't be pulled up very far if she were to fall.

Climber on lead with her belayer, Red Rocks, Nevada.

## Technique for belaying the leading climber

This technique is similar to belaying the top roped climber except that you will be paying out rope rather than taking in rope. The leading climber will be trailing the rope behind her as she climbs. Once the climber begins climbing, the belayer feeds out rope through the belay device—keeping pace with the climber's rate of ascent. The belayer's job is to pass just enough rope through the device so that the climber is trailing the rope effortlessly in her ascent. The climber should not feel any tugging of the rope. It is important, however, that the belayer also be careful not to pay out too much rope and create a loop of slack. If there were too much rope out between the belayer and the climber and the climber fell, it would result in a longer—possibly unsafe—fall.

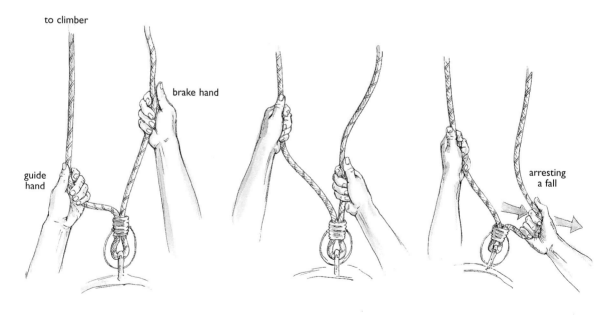

to climber

brake hand

guide
hand

arresting
a fall

**Belaying the lead climber.** When the climber is climbing, the belayer pays out rope at the pace of the climber's ascent. The belayer's guide hand feeds out rope by pulling it through the belay device; her brake hand, which is feeding the free end of the rope into the belay device, facilitates this. As in top rope belaying, the belayer's brake hand must always remain on the rope. To arrest the climber's fall, the belayer pulls her brake hand off to the outside.

## Multi-pitch climbing

Although not all that common, you may learn to climb by doing a multi-pitch route with your guide. Multi-pitch routes cannot be done with several people; it will be just you and your guide, rather than a group course. While more exciting in some aspects (height and exposure), I don't believe doing a multi-pitch route for your first climb is the most effective way to learn. There is simply too much to learn in a situation that is pretty intense. Unlike a group top rope class, you'll miss out on being able to practice newly learned techniques repeatedly on the same pitch, as well as on hearing other students' questions during the class.

## If you do a multi-pitch climb

Once at the base of the climb, your guide will let you know what to expect in terms of length of time on the route. She may recommend carrying a day pack or fanny pack for water and some food. Depending on the descent, you may carry your walking shoes

In **multi-pitch climbing**, the seconding climber is belayed from above by the leader, Java Dome, South Platte Area, Colorado.

on the back of your harness or in a pack. Most of the time you will leave your pack and extra gear at or near the base of the climb. All of these decisions will depend on the length of the route, the descent, and whether it is practical to return to the base of the route.

Before you or your guide gets off the ground, your guide will need to teach you to belay just as I've described on the previous page. Before she starts up the route, she'll also go over several other steps with you to make certain you're clear on the procedures. Here's how it'll go:

## Before the guide leaves the ground

You will be tied in—most likely with the figure 8 knot described in the previous indoor climbing section—and then tied off with either a clove hitch or a figure 8 on a bight (see pages 72–74) to an anchor point to prevent you from being pulled up in the case of a fall. The anchor could be a sling around a tree or attachment to natural gear at the base of the climb. Whatever the anchor, the rope that is tied to your harness will be attached to the anchor with a knot in the rope. Your guide also will demonstrate how to *clean* (see Cleaning the Pitch, page 70) the pitch as you follow and will give you a *nut tool* (see page 68) for the job.

# SOME WORDS YOU NEED TO KNOW

**Anchor** or **belay.** These two words are used interchangeably; however, in sport climbing or indoor climbing *anchor* is used more often. The anchor or belay of a route is the point where a climber can *safety* (secure) herself by tying into at least two protection points in order to belay her partner, the point where the top rope is attached, or the point where the climber will lower or rappel off the route. Some anchors are fixed, such as in bolted face climbs, where there are no features in which to place the removable type of protection, or in gyms, where all the top ropes are already set up in permanent anchors. Other anchors, usually those on traditional climbs, are crafted by the climber by using removable protection in features such as crack systems. Some anchors can even be natural features, such as a big tree or a boulder at the top of a cliff that can be tied off with webbing slings.

**Approach.** The *approach* is simply the hike to the crag. Sometimes the approach is as easy as walking 10 minutes on a flat, well-maintained trail, or it can entail steep scrambling over rocky terrain, such as talus fields. You'll often hear climbers ask, "What's the approach like?" The approach can be an important aspect in determining how early to get going in order to do a particular climb. Certainly if the approach is a lengthy and arduous one, you would also want to bring extra water.

**Biner (bee-ner).** This is short for *carabiner* and is commonly used. You'll rarely hear the full word *carabiner* used. See *carabiner* below for definition.

**Carabiner.** These are snap-link devices made of aluminum alloy. They are oval, D-shaped, or pear-shaped with a spring-loaded gate opening along one side. The gate is the hinged part that allows the climber to open the carabiner and attach it to things. Carabiners are used in a variety of ways, including attaching your belay device to your harness, clipping into belay anchors, attaching protection to your harness or gear sling, and attaching the rope to the protection points on a climb. They come in two types: locking and nonlocking. The locking carabiners, used for belaying or rappelling, have a

sleeve over the gate with a mechanism that locks the gate and prevents it from being opened accidentally.

**Crux.** The *crux* is the hardest section of a climb. It may be one or two moves or even a short section of several moves. Often, the difficulty of the crux, in addition to the overall intensity of the other moves and how well the route accepts pro, determines the grade of the climb.

**Draw.** See **Quickdraws** for definition. Although this case of word shortening is not as ubiquitous as *biner* for *carabiner*, it's still very common. Here, *draw* is used instead of *quickdraw*.

**Gear** (see *protection* below). This usually refers to the removable protection that a climber uses in traditional climbing. Items such as spring-loaded camming devices and wedge-shaped aluminum-wired stoppers are considered gear. This term is often used when asking about the nature of the protection points on a route: "What kind of gear does it take?" or "What's the gear like on that route?" You may also hear it used to describe how easy it is (or isn't) to find solid placements for the pro, as in "The gear is good [or bad] on that route."

**Gear sling.** This is a circular strap made of webbing that you wear over one shoulder and under the other arm (the same way you would wear a handbag that you didn't want stolen). This is how you carry the gear when on lead and where you put the gear when you're seconding and removing the pro that the leader has placed.

**Nut tool.** This is a flat metal tool with a hook at the end, which is used to help extract removable pro, and a hole at the other end, which is used for clipping it into the gear sling or harness with a carabiner. The nut tool is an essential item for anyone following a traditional route. It allows the seconding climber to reach into cracks and push the metal wedge part of wired nuts to dislodge them. It can also be helpful in reaching the trigger of a camming device that is set too deeply in a crack. Most people have a keeper cord tied to the non-hook end; this cord is clipped into the rope while cleaning to avoid dropping the tool accidentally.

**Piece.** The term *piece* is short for a piece of protection, and it usually refers to protection that has been placed in the rock rather than protection that is still hanging on the climber's gear sling. For example, you may hear, "It's a good thing the climbing was easy in that section because I was pretty far above my last piece."

**Pitch.** A *pitch* is a section of climbing from one belay to the next. A single-pitch route would be a climb from the ground only to an anchor point where the climb is finished. A multi-pitch route continues beyond the first anchor point (or belay). Multi-pitch routes are usually found on taller cliffs. Longer routes are broken up into multiple pitches because climbing ropes come in standard lengths of 50 to 60 meters (165 to 200 feet). It simply isn't possible to climb from the bottom to the top of a cliff in one pitch if the route is longer than the length of the rope. Not that each pitch is necessarily a full rope length, however—in fact, it rarely is. Usually the length of a pitch is determined by where the climber can find a natural stopping point to set up an anchor and to belay. For example, a pitch may be only 40 feet because there may be a nice ledge to stand on or a good place to set anchors.

**Protection** or **pro.** Again, the shortened version is preferred and is more commonly used. *Pro* refers to pieces of removable (or natural) protection points. (See the description of *gear* above because these words are synonymous.)

**Quickdraws.** *Quickdraws* are lengths of webbing that are sewn together and bar tacked in the middle with a carabiner attached to either end. This unit, the webbing plus carabiners, is used to clip into permanent bolts. It is also used to clip into other protection points to help the rope run smoothly. Quickdraws are usually the only *rack* (see below) a sport climber needs because the climber is only clipping into bolts.

**Rack.** A climber's *rack* is a selection of natural pro that would cover the range of sizes and types of cracks that the climber is going to encounter in traditional climbing. A rack can mean all the gear a climber owns, as in, "I've got two of every size stopper and camming device on my rack." Or, it can refer to the gear needed for a particular climb, as in, "I brought a pretty minimal rack because the route is easy and I've done it several times, so I know it doesn't take any small wires or small camming devices." The word *rack* can also be a verb describing how the gear is hung on the gear sling. Usually climbers rack their pro on the gear sling in order of type and size, with the smallest wired stoppers in the front and the largest camming devices in the back.

Kelley Jackson racking her gear in Tuolumne Meadows, Yosemite National Park.

## The guide finishes climbing the pitch

Once the guide has arrived at the end of the pitch, she will set up an anchor to safety herself. She'll then call down "off belay." When you hear that signal, you will de-rig the belay device by unlocking the carabiner and taking the rope out of the belay device. When the rope is free, you will call up "belay off," so that the guide knows that the rope is free. She will then begin pulling up the remaining rope, which will be lying at your feet.

## Preparing to climb

When the remaining rope is being pulled up, you will have a few moments to start getting ready. This is a good time to put your shoes on and to dismantle the anchor and untie the knot or knots that attached you to the anchor (see pages 72–74). Do *not* untie the figure 8 follow-through knot that attaches the rope to your harness; this *tie-in knot* remains tied into your harness until you're safely on the ground. When the rope comes tight to your harness or to the anchor you're tied into, you will call up "That's me." There is no need to feel rushed because this doesn't mean that the guide is ready for you to climb. Usually there is a short delay from the point when the rope is pulled up to when you can climb because the guide will need to rig her belay device and make certain the rope is getting laid out properly. You must wait until you hear her call down "belay on" before you begin climbing. Once you hear that and you're ready to go, you'll call up "climbing" so your guide knows to begin taking in rope through her belay device. In chapter 5, I discuss the actual movement of climbing in depth, so for the moment I'm going to skip over that and concentrate on the other aspects of your climb.

## Cleaning the pitch

Following or seconding means simply to climb on top rope with the belay from above, whereas the word *cleaning* describes what you do as you climb. A climb is protected with natural, removable pro, permanent bolts, or both. Cleaning natural pro takes a bit more skill than removing *quickdraws* from bolts that stay in the rock, which only entails unclipping the carabiner from the bolt. With the *camming devices*, you will simply pull back on the *triggers* located on the *stem*, which contracts the cams and allows you to remove the unit. Wired *stoppers* are wedged in the rock; some fiddling is often required to get them out of the cracks. The *nut tool* can be used to hit a stopper to loosen it from the crack it's sitting in.

Once you have removed the pro from the rock, the next step is to unclip it from the rope and clip it onto the gear loops that are on the side of your harness or onto a gear sling worn over your shoulder. As you progress up the route, you will remove all of the gear on the route; the amount of gear hanging from your harness or gear sling will grow. Be aware that taking pro out of the rock can be a bit tricky and isn't always as easy as it sounds. If you get stuck and can't seem to get the pro out, let your guide know. She'll probably remember how she put the piece in and can talk you through how to remove it.

Rappelling with a figure 8.

## At the belay

On easy routes, the anchor or belay is usually at some sort of ledge or at least a *stance* (a place where you can stand). On occasion, there won't be a stance, and you'll have to sit suspended in your harness off the anchors (called a *hanging belay*). When you arrive at the anchor, your guide will tie you directly in so that she can take you off belay. She will then de-rig her belay device and begin taking the pro that's now on your harness from you. Then she'll have you put her on belay again, so she can lead the next pitch. You may not feel completely confident in newly learned skills such as rigging the belay device just yet; however, any such activities will be supervised by the guide to ensure that you're doing them correctly.

### Climbing the second pitch

The only thing that differs now that you're belaying from a pitch off the ground is that once the guide has led the next pitch and gets to the part where she will be pulling up the remaining rope, you cannot dismantle the belay until you hear her say "belay on." That is, when the rope becomes tight and you say "that's me," the rope will be tight to the anchor rather than to your harness directly. You must wait until you hear the signal "belay on" before you can unclip or take any of the anchors out.

## Getting back down

Once you reach the top of the route, more than likely you will walk off the top of the cliff. There may be some routes that require rappels to get back down; this is usually the case when there is no option of walking off. Rappelling is a lot like being lowered, but you control the descent yourself. The device you've used for belaying is also what you use for rappelling. You probably won't rappel during your first climb, because usually the first time you rappel, you need to be backed up with a top rope. On a multi-pitch climb, this simply may not be practical. If the descent does require a rappel, the guide will lower you and then rappel herself. This is the safest method.

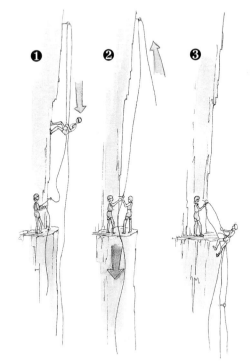

**Multi-pitch rappelling 1.** Rappelling to a rappel anchor. **2.** Pulling the rope from the previous anchor and setting it up for the next rappel. **3.** Continuing the rappel.

## THREE KNOTS
· · · · · · · · · · · · · · · · · · · · · · · · · · · · · · · · · · · · · · · · · · · · · · · · · · · · · · · · · · ·

Attaching yourself to the anchor is done by tying a knot into the rope fairly close to your tie-in knot. The distance the knot is out from the tie-in point varies depending on how close or how far away from the anchor points you want to be—typically 1 to 4 feet. These are the three most common knots used to clip into an anchor.

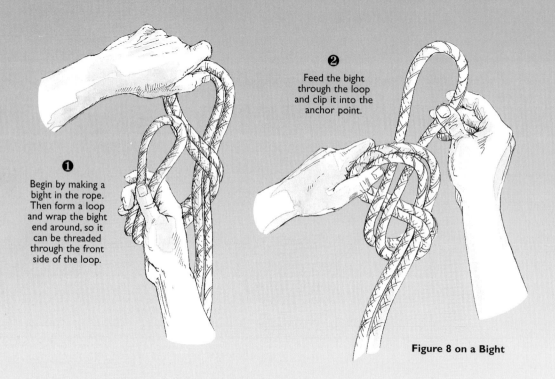

❷ Feed the bight through the loop and clip it into the anchor point.

❶ Begin by making a bight in the rope. Then form a loop and wrap the bight end around, so it can be threaded through the front side of the loop.

**Figure 8 on a Bight**

**Figure 8 on a bight.** This knot is most common. It's easy to learn because it's similar to the figure 8 tie-in knot and its shape makes it quick to recognize when it's tied correctly (or incorrectly). The "bight" (another word for bend) part of the finished knot is what you will clip into the carabiners of the anchor. Since most anchors have more than one point of protection, you will tie a separate knot for each point that you clip into.

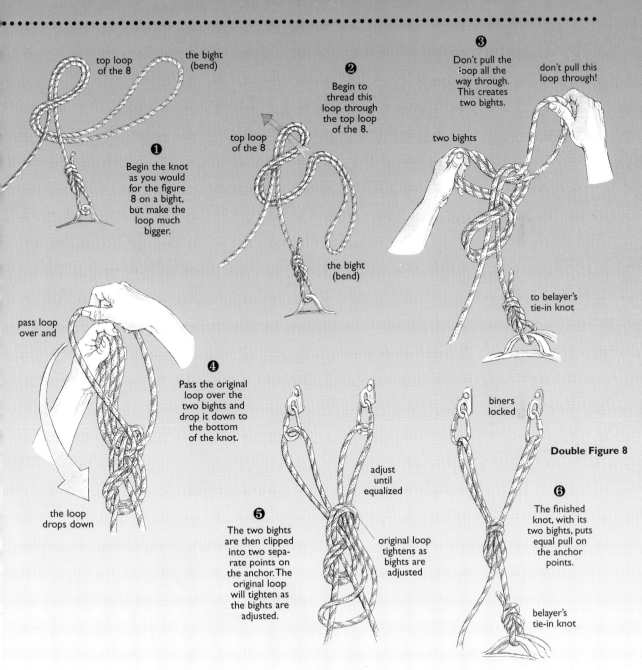

**1** Begin the knot as you would for the figure 8 on a bight, but make the loop much bigger.

top loop of the 8

the bight (bend)

**2** Begin to thread this loop through the top loop of the 8.

top loop of the 8

the bight (bend)

**3** Don't pull the loop all the way through. This creates two bights.

don't pull this loop through!

two bights

to belayer's tie-in knot

pass loop over and

the loop drops down

**4** Pass the original loop over the two bights and drop it down to the bottom of the knot.

**5** The two bights are then clipped into two separate points on the anchor. The original loop will tighten as the bights are adjusted.

adjust until equalized

original loop tightens as bights are adjusted

biners locked

**Double Figure 8**

**6** The finished knot, with its two bights, puts equal pull on the anchor points.

belayer's tie-in knot

**Double (Bight) Figure 8.** With this knot, two bights are formed so that you can clip into two separate anchor points and equalize the amount of pull on those points.

## THREE KNOTS (continued)

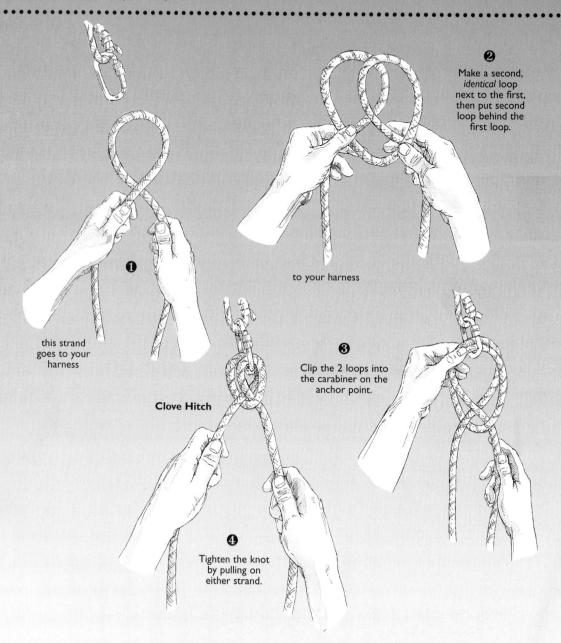

❶ this strand goes to your harness

❷ Make a second, *identical* loop next to the first, then put second loop behind the first loop.

to your harness

**Clove Hitch**

❸ Clip the 2 loops into the carabiner on the anchor point.

❹ Tighten the knot by pulling on either strand.

**Clove hitch.** This is a wonderful knot because it is very easy to tie, doesn't take up much rope, and can be adjusted (that is, you can change your distance away from the anchor) without having to untie it. To adjust the clove hitch, loosen the knot, then feed one of the strands in the direction you'd like to lengthen (or shorten), and pull the other strand to retighten the knot.

# Chapter 5

# MOVEMENT: THE REALLY FUN PART OF CLIMBING

At last we get to the best part of climbing: the climbing itself. Once you've learned the safety drills covered in chapter 4, they become the background for the true art form in climbing—the movement. Movement draws most people to the sport and is the focus of nearly everything climbers do to improve. Rock climbing movement, when done well, is like an exquisitely choreographed dance. It can be delicate or dynamic, graceful or gymnastic—or all of these things at once.

> Rock climbing movement, when done well, is like an exquisitely choreographed dance.

And the dance is always changing; each route you do will require different choreography, so you'll need to be creative and strategic in your movements. Over time, you'll develop a repertoire of movements and will begin to recognize when to use them. The best climbers in the world are able to execute and link their movements with style and elegance. They have the ability to make very difficult climbs look easy.

In chapter 4, I emphasized the importance of learning the basics from a qualified instructor. However, in truth, it is a rare introductory class or instructor that can teach you much about how to move well over rock. It isn't that the instructor doesn't know how to teach this but that the primary goal is to teach you how to be safe first. After that, the time left over for instruction on the intricacies of movement is limited. This chapter is designed to help you go beyond what you will be taught in your first basic course. Take these ideas with you to your first class; then reread this chapter afterward. It will make more sense after you've climbed once.

When you're first starting out, you should always be climbing on top rope. This way you can relax and not worry about falling. Remember that if you fall on top rope, you don't really fall any distance but instead you just weight the rope, which is always above you. Your focus can be entirely on your footwork, your balance, and the sequence of movements as well as on breathing and staying relaxed.

It's important that you start out on an easy route—around 5.5 to 5.6 is a good level for a beginner. Again, you want to be able to focus on the climbing and enjoy the experience. If you start out on a route that is too hard, you'll just be frustrated and your ability to learn will be limited. This same strategy applies even past that first day or first month of climbing. Whenever you're learning something new or trying to improve a certain technique, you should be on a route that isn't taxing you beyond your ability to think and focus. I often see people on routes that are so far above their current ability level that they simply cannot learn *anything*; their minds are consumed with the desperate struggle to just hang on.

The first time you get on a wall, your greatest challenge as a beginner will be to ignore your instinct or your preconceived ideas about climbing. Two factors are at play here: an innate fear of falling, and the fact that the movement of climbing as an adult is no longer natural, as it was when you were a kid. I cannot tell you that it is going to be easy to rise above these things, but I do have a suggestion that might help: focus on one or two of the concepts from this chapter and commit yourself to them during your first lesson. If you can do this in spite of your natural instinct to do otherwise, you will be far ahead of the game.

## BASIC CONCEPTS OF MOVEMENT

You can break down climbing movement into two types: face climbing and crack climbing.

*Face climbing* technique, which is what we're going to tackle first, is by far the most natural movement of climbing. For this reason, it's usually the type of climbing that most people start with. However, the fact that it's more natural doesn't necessarily mean that it will be completely instinctual. In this chapter I address the fundamentals of good face climbing technique in a way that will correlate with your initial experience on a wall. I move from basic concepts to more complex techniques and how to use specific holds.

All of the concepts of movement that I describe for face climbing will also serve you in *crack climbing* (technique for ascending cracks, described later in this chapter) situations. The essential components of learning to move over rock—balance, footwork, body positioning, conservation of energy (especially in the arms), precision, and fluidity of movement—are the same regardless of the type of climbing you're doing. Also, no matter what level you attain in this sport, you'll find that these techniques will be the bedrock of *all* your climbing movement—even for the more advanced techniques I cover in chapter 6. Your progress in this sport will be essentially a honing and refinement of these basic skills. I encourage you to reread these sections from time to time because you can always improve by going back to these original concepts.

> **T**he most elementary rule of climbing: keep your weight over your feet.

The concepts of keeping your weight over your feet, maintaining balance in your movements, and using as little upper body strength as possible are the same for both face and crack climbing. However, crack climbing also requires very specific, and sometimes tricky, techniques that are not terribly natural. The techniques are based on the concepts of wedging, jamming, and torquing various body parts into a crack. Most often the body parts are the hands, fingers, and feet although even knees, elbows, or the entire body can come into play. Crack climbing is definitely a learned art—and the learning process to master this art is rarely a speedy one. It takes quite a bit of practice along with a good dose of humility and tolerance for pain to become a competent crack climber. Once you do learn the techniques, however, it is an extremely fun and gratifying form of climbing. If you start out in an area that is mainly a crack climbing area, don't despair. Most crack climbs of an easy grade will offer you as much opportunity to use face climbing techniques as to use pure crack techniques.

## BASIC TECHNIQUES: FACE CLIMBING

All climbing is primarily done with the feet and legs, not with the arms and hands, because the upper body is relatively weak compared to the lower body. So, at every possible moment, you should be standing on your feet and using your legs to push you up the climb. To succeed at this, you must follow the most elementary rule of climbing: keep your weight over your feet—your body must be positioned so that your weight is centered directly over your feet. When I speak about weight, I mean your mass or your center of gravity. The angle of the wall you're climbing will govern your body position. For the moment, I'll talk about climbs that are not overhanging, because this is the type of terrain a beginner will learn on.

Typically the climbs you'll learn on will be less than vertical. If you begin outside, the cliff will be at a lower angle than you might find indoors, but your body position is about the same whether the angle is 60 degrees or closer to 90. The ideal body position is upright with your torso away from the wall. Picture your body oriented vertically just as it would be if you were climbing a ladder or even stairs. You wouldn't lean into the angle of the stairs or the ladder; you would keep the same posture as you would simply standing on the ground. This is how to keep your weight over your feet and remain in balance. Many beginners have a tendency to lean into the rock with their bodies, with the misguided notion that clinging to the wall will ensure that they will not be pried loose from it. Unfortunately, this has quite the opposite effect; the more you lean into the wall, the less weight is on your feet, and you will experience the nerve-racking sensation of your feet sliding out from underneath you.

**Mental trick:** When you feel stressed, your arms feel pumped, or you're just not sure what to do next, *look down for a better way to use your feet.*

## Focus on your feet

As you first pull onto the wall, the most important thing to remember is this: use your feet! I cannot emphasize enough the importance of this one thing. However, for the most part, beginners ignore the footholds and focus mainly on the handholds. In fact, they often have the tendency to overgrip the handholds as they look up for the next one to grab, rarely looking down at where to put their feet next. If you feel as if you're only looking up, frantically searching for the next handhold, you need to shift your focus to your feet and the footholds. Looking down for foot placements sounds like a very simple thing to do, but it is one of the most common errors I see in beginning climbers and even in intermediate climbers. By contrast, the top rock climbers you see look down at their feet more than they look up.

### Placing your feet precisely

There is more to using your feet, however, than simply finding the footholds and plopping your feet onto them. After you've looked down and seen where your foothold is, the next step is to be precise with your foot placement. Many people, beginners and intermediates alike, rely on their eye-to-foot coordination to get their foot onto the hold. That is, they look at the hold for an instant, begin to place their foot on it, and just as the foot is about to land on the hold they look up again to their hands. In the extreme, the climber hardly glances at the hold and her foot actually drags down the wall before landing (if she's lucky) on the foothold. As you can imagine, this invariably leads to poor foot placement. To have good footwork and to take the best advantage of the holds, you must make a concerted effort to follow your foot with your eyes until it is firmly on the hold. Only when you actually *see* that you're using the best part of your shoe on the best part of the hold should you look away from your foot.

### How to use footholds

How you place your feet on the holds is also crucial to how well the holds will work for you. The type of foothold will determine exactly how you'll position your foot. There are essentially three ways to use your feet on holds in face climbing: edging, smearing, and toeing-in (see page 79). For all of these foot positions remember the following: you want to keep your heel lower than your toe. This is the most relaxed position for your calf muscles. Here is a basic guide to help you determine how to use your feet on different holds.

**Mental trick:** Train yourself to look down instead of up by repeating a little mantra: *"Look down for footholds, not up for handholds."*

· · · · · · · · · · · · · · · · · · · · · · · · · · · · · · · · · · · · · · · · · · · · · · · · · ·

**Mental trick:** To make sure you're always putting your foot on the hold correctly and precisely, train yourself to "keep your eye on the toe," just as you would "keep your eye on the ball" in other sports. Your mantra could be something like, "My eyes stay with my foot until it's on the hold."

· · · · · · · · · · · · · · · · · · · · · · · · · · · · · · · · · · · · · · · · · · · · · · · · · ·

## Edging

The most common type of foot placement is *edging*. You will *edge* on any hold that has a positive protrusion, whether it's an edge with a flat surface or a slight rib that is sloping downward from the plane of the wall. The holds you'll edge on don't necessarily have to be "edges"; edging technique can be used on any hold that is sticking *out* from the wall. For example, on a knoblike hold or a rounded bump you will probably still edge. You'll use the front part of your foot on the hold

Edging.

rather than the ball of your foot or your arch. Your objective will be to utilize the front section of your shoe right under your big toe on is *inside edge* (the left side of your right big toe, the right side of your left big toe). It is on this inside edge of your big toe that most of your climbing will be done on. Your foot will be positioned at about a 45-degree angle from the plane of the wall. Later on, as the angle gets steeper, you'll also learn to use the *outside edge* of your shoe (the part closer to your small toe); I cover this in chapter 6.

## Smearing

On *slab climbs* (low-angle face climbs), you may not use a specific hold, such as an edge, but rather will *smear* the foot onto depressions or other subtle irregularities of the rock. This technique requires you to find areas on the wall that have a slight scoop or dish, which creates an even lower angle than the surrounding rock. Sometimes you will smear in the area just above a very fine, dime-thin edge, if the overall angle of the rock is very gentle. Finding the right place to step for smearing takes some practice and a sharp eye. These foot placements work by *smearing* as much of the sole of your shoe on the given area while applying your full weight over your foot. Usually,

**Top:** More of the sole of the shoe is used in smearing. **Above:** Toeing-in is typically used in pockets or other inward-type footholds.

**Mental trick:** When you feel as if the next hold is just out of reach or you're not able to pull any more with your arms, *think about pushing more with your legs.* Even use a mental chant to yourself: *push, push, push with those feet!*

you will use the entire front part of the shoe, sometimes as far back as the ball of the foot. Your foot stays on because of the friction between the rock and the sole of your shoe. The force you place on the smear creates this friction, so it is paramount that your balance is directly over your feet when smearing. Smearing is a delicate and sometimes tenuous type of footwork. However, it is an easily acquired skill because the sensation of a successful smear is readily felt. With experience, you will learn to spot where you can smear and know just what position your foot and body need to be in to make the smear work.

## Toeing-in

You will usually use a *toeing-in* technique on holds called *pockets*. Pockets are simply holds that don't stick out from the wall but are instead holes in the rock. Pockets and other inward holds will require you to place your foot pointing more or less straight in with the foot perpendicular to the wall. The trickiest part of using pockets for your feet is that these types of holds are not easily seen once you're above them. For this reason, it's important that you not get too stretched out between your handholds and your footholds. You'll want to place your feet a little higher relative to your handholds than you normally would when using footholds that stick out from the rock.

Whatever type of footwork you use—edging, smearing, or toeing-in—you'll mainly be on your toes. This will give you the most precision, as well as the most power to push with.

## Standing on your feet, pushing with your legs

Once your focus is on the footholds and you've succeeded in getting your feet on them precisely, your goal is to use your legs to push you up the route. To do that, you must really have your weight over your feet. Always try to position yourself, your center of mass, over your feet—really *stand* on your feet. Then, very consciously, use your legs to push you to the next holds. Think of it as a leg press. This is quite the opposite of pulling with your arms, which you may be tempted to do. Be assured your legs are much stronger than your arms are, so you'll want to enlist their help as much as possible to save strength in your upper body.

• • • • • • • • • • • • • • • • • • • • • • • • • • •

**Mental trick:** When the footholds become very small, *think about what position your body needs to be in to put the most force on your feet.*

• • • • • • • • • • • • • • • • • • • • • • • • • • •

### Trusting your feet and committing your weight to them

To figure out where to put your feet so you can push, remember that anything that you used for your hands will ultimately become your foothold. In addition, you can also make use of really small holds for your feet that would be impossible to use with your hands. You'll be amazed at what tiny holds your feet can stand on. It simply requires that you trust your feet and really commit your weight to the holds you're on. Remember: the rubber on your climbing shoes is very soft and sticky; given the correct angles and pressure, your shoes can adhere with friction alone, even where there are no holds. Use your imagination: look for edges, nubbins, divots, small depressions, any place that would allow you some purchase on the rock. Then step onto the hold and totally commit your weight to it.

This weight commitment is the only way to make very small footholds work: if you only partially weight the hold, your foot will want to slip off. The full pressure of your weight keeps you on the hold. Many beginners try to test whether a foothold is any good by placing a foot on the hold *without weighting it*; when the foot slips off, they give up on the hold. Ironically, the foothold probably didn't work *because* they didn't weight it. The only way to truly test whether your foot will stay on a hold is to totally commit your weight to it.

In order to weight the footholds, you must put direct downward pressure on them. On walls that are lower angle (less than vertical), you'll need to stand straight down on the footholds with your body away from the rock. If you lean into the wall with your body—which, by the way, will be your very human instinct to do—you'll create a situation where your feet have less weight on them and they'll be likely to slip out from under you.

### Using your body

Climbing with your body in balance is the most energy-efficient way to climb. If you find you're pulling a lot with your arms to make the next move or if you feel that if you let go to move one of your limbs, you're just going to swing right off the other holds, you're probably not moving in balance. When you let go of a hold to reach to the next, the other hand and your feet must some-

To climb in balance, think of "opposing forces" in your points of contact. When you're making a move upward where one hand is reaching to the next hold, the most balanced way to move is by pushing with one foot while the opposite hand is pulling on a hold. To understand this, imagine your body divided into quadrants. In the illustration, the ideal position for moving to the next handhold would be for the climber to have the points of contact be the hand in quadrant B opposed by the foot in quadrant C. Likewise, if the hand in quadrant A were the one holding and pulling, the foot in quadrant D would be pushing to help it.

**The** only way to test whether your foot will stay on a hold is to totally commit your weight to it.

how remain in balance so that you can make the move with as little effort as possible.

### Staying in balance as you move

When you coordinate the pulling of your hands and pushing of your feet, balancing action and reaction, you are said to be *moving in balance*. Up to this point, I've talked about how important your *feet* are, but the truth is, it's usually one *foot* that does more pushing than the other foot. And which foot that is depends on which hand is reaching to the next hold. I can translate this to you two ways. The first way is what I call *opposite hand to foot*—while one hand is reaching for the next hold, the other hand will be pulling on a hold while its opposite foot is pushing on a hold (for example, if the right hand is pulling, then the left foot is pushing). Or you can think of it like this: if you're reaching up with one hand, then it will be the foot on that same side of your body that will be doing most of the work of pushing you up the route. Using the example at left: reaching with the left hand means the left foot will be pushing on the hold. This is because the left foot is helping the right hand—the left foot and the right hand are balancing each other.

You can also think of your body in terms of quadrants. Draw an imaginary line vertically, splitting the left and right sides of your body. Then draw a line through your waist. To move in balance, when your hand in quadrant A is reaching for a hold, your two points of contact that are most important to your balance will be your foot in quadrant C and your hand in quadrant B.

### Biggest isn't always best

This concept of climbing in balance is also about how you relate your entire body to the available holds on the climb. Many climbers—especially those just starting out—will gravitate toward the biggest handholds and footholds, regardless of whether they are in balance while using those holds. It is more important to choose holds that keep you in balance rather than just reaching for the biggest holds available. As you choose your next hold, you should be assessing your body's state of equilibrium: Will putting my weight onto this foothold require a lot of strength to compensate for how out of balance I become? Is there a smaller, less obvious hold that I could use that will keep my center of gravity over my feet?

What I'm describing is a sensation you will feel. It takes more than just seeing a hold and grabbing it. Finding the best holds (not only the biggest) to use on a climb requires you to be keenly aware of your entire body as it moves from hold to hold. Choose holds that are in the right place to give you the needed weight distribution or balance, rather than the ones that are the easiest to grab.

## Not too high, not too low

• • • • • • • • • • • • • • • • • • • • • • • • •

Finding the best holds (not only the biggest) to use on a climb requires you to be keenly aware of your entire body as it moves from hold to hold.

• • • • • • • • • • • • • • • • • • • • • • • • •

**Mental trick:** Remind yourself to take a moment to really look around at the available footholds. Often beginners will see only holds of a certain size, remaining totally blind to small but perfectly useful footholds. Ask yourself: Have I *really* considered all the options?

• • • • • • • • • • • • • • • • • • • • • • • • •

Where your feet are relative to your hands is yet another aspect of climbing in balance. If you get your feet too high, your center of gravity (a polite way of saying "your butt") will be hanging out in space, putting more weight on your arms. Then, if you do manage to stand up on your legs, you end up with your handholds too low, which is also taxing on your arms. Likewise, keeping your feet too low can cause problems. Because your arms are above you and totally extended, you can't really push yourself back away from the wall to look down to find your next foot placement. Try to use footholds that allow your arm position, as they are gripping the handholds, to be somewhere in the middle of the spectrum from fully extended to fully bent.

## Small steps

Whether you're face climbing or crack climbing, it's always best to take small steps rather than big ones. Again, you may be tempted to step from one big foothold to the next big foothold, bypassing the small ones in between—but don't! Lifting your foot very high will put more pressure on your hands and arms because it throws your weight back, away from the wall. It's much more efficient to move upward with your feet in small increments. I've also found that, when I feel I'm a little too short and the next handhold is just out of reach, sometimes all I need to do is

Stemming is one of the most perfect examples of how important opposition can be. In a stemmed position, the feet are pushing against the holds rather than pressing downward on them. Stemming is an excellent way to make moves less strenuous, since it takes weight off your arms and is also useful as a secure position when clipping on lead and resting between moves. Calaveras Dome, California.

take one little baby step up and I've made the move. (From time to time, you may step your foot up to a very high foothold and then rock your weight onto it, a move called a *high step*, but this is only used when there are no other options for your feet.)

## Types of moves using your entire body

### Stemming

Being efficient in your climbing also means saving strength in your arms whenever possible. *Stemming* is a fantastic strength-saving position that can be used for resting as well as for upward progress. Instead of looking for holds that are oriented horizontally that you can grasp and pull down on or step onto with your feet and push, you will look for holds that are oriented vertically and that oppose each other, so that you can push against them. The classic use of stemming is seen in chimney climbing or *dihedrals* (sections of rock where two walls come together to form an angle, such as the inside corner of a room), where the climber is using the two opposite walls with her legs bridged between them (see photo).

In face climbing, particularly in steep face climbing, you can use stemming to conserve the strength in your arms. Because your body weight is suspended between the two holds that your feet are pressing against, this position takes a lot of the weight off your arms.

Getting into a stem requires that you find two holds that you can push laterally against with your feet a fair distance apart. Imagine that your legs are forming an inverted "V" from your hips down; the wider the "V," the more weight that is taken off your arms. Stemming also requires a commitment to push very hard on your feet; this is especially true if the holds you're pushing against aren't that *positive*, that is, big or secure. Remember that these holds you're using wouldn't work at all if it weren't for the opposition created by your two feet pushing against them.

Making upward progress with stemming requires the use of your hands as well as your feet. Since both feet are creating the opposition that makes stemming work, in order to move one foot upward, you must be able to take the weight off that foot without diminishing the *push* (force of pressure) against the other foot. You can do this by replacing the opposing force of one of your feet with one or both of your hands. To move one foot, you may push downward and sideways with the palm of your hand (on the same side as the moving foot) to replace the pushing that was done by that foot. Your other hand may be holding onto a downward-pulling type of hold. In the situation of a dihedral or chimney, you may be pushing with both of your hands against the opposite walls to free up a foot.

## Lie backing

*Lie backing*, like stemming, relies on the forces of opposition to work. It is often used when climbing a crack in a corner or where there is a vertical edge on a face. The climber's hands pull outward on the edge of a hold while the feet press against the wall. The most efficient way to lie back is to keep the arms as straight as possible and to make small upward moves. The climber's feet will usually be quite high, much closer to the hands than in straight-on face climbing. This is definitely the best position if there are no real footholds and if the feet are being held in place by the opposing force of the pulling of the arms. Even though, traditionally, lie back technique is associated with crack climbing, it can be invaluable on face climbs as a technique for getting past sections where there seem to be no footholds. If you find a positive vertical edge but don't see any usable footholds, you can lie back the edge with your hands and smear your feet on the wall; this pull-push will let you advance to the next holds. I won't kid you: steep and sustained lie back climbing can be strenuous. This is especially true when you're just learning it.

## Mantling

This maneuver is usually encountered on slab climbs, not on overhanging climbs. You'll use *mantling* to get your feet established on a handhold where there are few or no intermediate holds leading up to it and the handholds above it are too far out of reach. More commonly, you'll also use mantling to gain a ledge or to top out on a boulder problem, which I discuss below.

When you're lie backing an edge **(top)** or lie backing a crack **(above)**, the principles are the same: your feet push against the wall, while your hands pull outward on the holds.

You'll start out with your hands on a hold above you. Then you'll walk your feet partway up while pulling yourself up to a point where you can change your hands from their downward

Executing a **mantle**.

pulling position to a pushing position with the palms of your hands on the hold instead. It is this transition from pulling to pushing that is the most difficult; on certain climbs, where there aren't even tiny footholds to take some of the weight off your arms, this can be a pretty strenuous move. It helps to try to get the mass of your upper body over your palms. Once your palms are on the hold, you'll then push yourself up as high as you can, trying to straighten your arms, and then lift one foot onto the hold where your hands are. You'll want to make sure before you start into the mantle that you have saved enough room on the hold to put a foot beside your hand. Then you'll rock your weight over that foot and stand up on it. The standing up part can also be tricky, especially if the hold is narrow, the wall above the hold is fairly steep, or you can't yet reach the handholds on the slope above you. It is the quintessential balancing act to get your weight over your foot and press up on it at the same time.

Pure mantles are not that common; however, you'll find the mantling technique very useful for getting onto ledges or onto the top of boulder problems. In these more common situations, there will be no wall above you, so you'll have no holds above to grab. Often, beginners get into trouble in this situation because they start reaching and leaning forward, searching for something to grab onto with their hands. At that point, they can no longer see (or use) their feet, and in an act of desperation they flop themselves onto the ledge like a beached whale. Not very dignified, nor very efficient. Instead, you'll want do exactly what I've described above for mantling: keep your hands nearer to the edge. You'll find that because there is no wall or slope above you, rocking your weight and your upper body over your foot will be much easier than in a pure mantle.

## How to use different handholds

I've hardly mentioned what to do with your hands because using the handholds will be more intuitive and because, honestly, it's less important to your success on the route than what you do with your feet and your body position. However, below I describe the types of handholds you'll encounter and how to use your hands, your fingers, and the rest of your body in relation to these holds.

## Edge

An *edge* can be as wide as your entire hand or as thin as a dime. When climbers refer to edges for handholds, though, they usually mean something that is anywhere from ⅛ of an inch to 1½ inches thick. An edge can be completely flat or can have a lip that makes it possible to pull out on it, not just down on it. There are two ways to hold an edge: crimping and an open-hand grip.

**Left:** Big edges are usually taken open-handed. **Below:** Crimping an edge. **Bottom:** Pinch hold.

*Crimping* is a way of holding the edge with your fingertips flat on the hold and your fingers arched over them. For additional strength in crimping, your thumb should be on top of the index finger.

On bigger edges, where you can get more of your hand on the hold, you may use an *open-hand grip*. (See "Sloper" below for more on the open-hand grip.) Whether you crimp or hold the edge openhanded, use your thumb on the hold whenever possible because it is your strongest digit. Also, keep your fingers together, not spread apart, because this also helps strengthen your grip.

## Pinch

A *pinch* is a hold that is gripped by pinching it between the thumb and the rest of the fingers. Pinches can be small, where your thumb and fingers are close together, or they can be really wide, with the hand almost completely open. How easy pinches are to hold depends on the size of your hand relative to the hold.

## Pocket

A *pocket* is a hole in the rock where you can insert a finger, or two or three. Pockets range in both the size of the opening and the depth. They take a little getting used to, especially in the one- and two-finger varieties, because there is more stress on the tendons and joints when your fingers are so

isolated. When you encounter a one- or two-finger pocket, use your strongest fingers first: your middle finger for one-digit pockets and your middle and ring finger for two-finger pockets.

## Sloper

A *sloper* is a hold that is rounded and slopes down without the benefit of a positive edge. Slopers are some of the most difficult holds to learn how to use. They require an open-hand grip, which is the opposite of crimping. Holding slopers requires a unique kind of strength coupled with the friction between your hand and the hold. When you reach up to take a sloper, you'll need to really feel around for the best part of the hold and then completely wrap your hand on the hold, fingers held together. This is one of the rare times you're likely to use your palm on a hold. Keep in mind that slopers are easier to hold when they are above you and you're able to keep your arms straight when holding them; they feel worse when you pull up on them.

## Side pull

A *side pull* is typically an edge that is vertically oriented or slightly diagonal. This is a hold that you will not be able to pull straight down on. You make a side pull work by opposing your hands and your feet. With your hand pulling outward on the hold, you'll push your feet in the opposite direction; this opposition makes the hold work. A side pull is normally taken with the palm facing inward and the thumb up.

**Far left: Side pull**, Boulder Mountain Park, Colorado. **Center: Gaston hold. Below:** Climber using an **undercling** on a flake.

## Gaston

A *gaston* (pronounced *gas-tone*) is named for a famous French climber from the 1960s, Gaston Rebuffat. The hold's name originated from an old photo of Rebuffat using this technique to climb a crack. Ironically, the gaston is just about the worst technique you can use for crack climbing; however, it works brilliantly in other situations. A gaston is similar to a side pull in that it is vertically or diagonally oriented. Like a side pull, it requires that you use opposition with your feet to make it work. A gaston is taken with your palm facing away from you with the thumb down.

## Undercling

An *undercling* is a hold that you take from underneath, with your palm facing upward. It can be an edge, a pocket, or a *flake*—a flake is a thin plate of rock separated from the main part of the rock; the separation allows a climber's hands to use it. Undercling holds tend to be easier to use the higher your body is in relation to the hold. If you grab an undercling above your head, it may feel terrible. However, that same undercling taken at waist level could feel very positive. So, whenever possible, move up quickly into undercling holds to make better use of them. If there aren't many footholds, underclinging will be another exercise in using opposition. You will pull outward on the undercling with your palms up, while you push (smear) your feet against the rock. You'll also want to keep your arms as straight as possible because this is the most efficient way to conserve strength in what is already a fairly strenuous type of move.

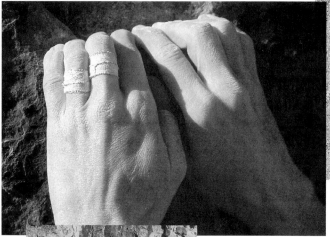

**Above:** Climber **palming** while in a stemmed position. **Left:** Matching hands. **Bottom left:** Getting a **shake** (see page 92) on a steep climb can make the difference between success and failure.

## Palming

*Palming* is a great energy-saving technique. Instead of pulling down on an edge, you use the heel of your hand to push downward on a hold that is below your chest level. Palming is often used to take weight off one foot to lift it to the next foothold (as in stemming). The move saves strength because you're resting your weight on your hand rather than pulling on a hold that's above you.

## Matching

*Matching* is sometimes necessary when you need to change hands (or feet) on a certain hold. On big holds, it's pretty easy because you'll be able to fit both hands and feet on the hold quite easily. On small holds, matching becomes trickier. For your handholds, you'll need to think ahead and save room on the hold for your other hand. In extreme situations, you may even have to lift one finger off at a time while you replace it with one from your other hand. For footholds, often you'll need to switch feet on very small holds where it is impossible to share the hold with both feet. In this situation, you'll need to put the newly arriving foot just above the toe of the departing foot and then squirm the departing foot off the hold while the new foot slides in to replace it. You can also do a kind of hop-step, where you take the weight off the departing foot in a little hop while the arriving foot hops onto the hold.

### IMPORTANCE OF RESTING

To climb, you must not only master the movement but also what happens *between* the moves you make. A good climber is not only efficient in her moves, but she also knows how to use the least

## CLIMBING SLANG

· · · · · · · · · · · · · · · · · · · · · · · · · · · · · · · · · · · · · · · · · · · · · · · · · · · · · · · · · · · ·

Here are some words that you will undoubtedly hear at the crag or in the gym.

- **Barn-door effect.** The result of a climber getting out of balance, causing the body to swing out away from the wall like a barn door opening.

- **Beta.** The information on how a route should be climbed, what holds to look out for, what body position works best, and so on. If you tell someone how to do specific moves, you're giving them beta.

- **Body tension.** A key ingredient when climbing on steep walls and roofs. The best climbers will always be able to keep their torso and legs under a constant amount of tension but still be able to breathe evenly and stay relaxed at the same time. Body tension keeps the body in a controlled position while the climber is moving from one hold to another; thus, the climber can make full use of the opposing forces of her feet pushing onto the holds and of her arms pulling on the holds.

- **Bomber.** Any hold that is extremely solid and easy to use. Short for *bombproof*. Protection can also be bomber, which means that it is very sound (a bomb could go off and it would still hold).

- **Bouldery.** Used to describe moves on a route that are difficult and powerful, such as moves found on boulder problems. If a route has a short section of climbing that is substantially harder than the rest of the route, it's deemed *bouldery*.

- **Bucket** (or **jug**). A big hold—or one that allows outward pull by the hands, not just downward pull, known as an *in-cut*—that you can really get your hand into or around.

- **Crank.** To powerfully pull through to a hold.

- **Crimper.** A small hold, just big enough for the fingertips, which you have to crimp your fingers to hold on to. A climb with lots of crimpers is *crimpy*.

- **Crux.** The hardest part of a climb. The section on a route where the climber is likely to fall or have the most trouble negotiating the moves.

- **Deadpoint.** A type of dynamic move wherein you use momentum to generate the upward movement and then grab the hold you're shooting for at the precise moment before the body starts to come back down. That moment of weightlessness is called the *deadpoint*.

- **Deck.** As a noun: the ground. As a verb: to fall to the ground.

- **Dirt me.** Lower me.

- **Dyno.** A lunge for a faraway hold. This is different from a deadpoint because the feet can easily fly off in this move. Sometimes also called a *lunge*, it's the opposite of a controlled, "static" move.

- **Flash.** Leading a climb and finishing in one push, without ever falling or hanging on the rope. This differs from an on-sight flash (see below) in that, here, the climber had crucial information (or beta) on how to do the moves.

- **Grease.** Slipping off a hold, usually because the hold was a sloper, the climber's hands were sweaty, or both.

- **Gripped.** Paralyzed with fear.

- **Jug.** *Jug* is slang for a really big hold.

- **On-sight.** Getting to the top of a route on the very first attempt without falling and while having no prior information on the moves of the route. This is considered the very best style of an ascent. Abbreviated form of *on-sight flash*.

- **Pro or piece.** Short for a piece of protection, which usually refers only to removable gear placements, such as stoppers and cams, rather than bolts.

- **Pumped.** When a climber's arms are pumped full of lactic acid, leading ultimately to an inability to hold on. A really steep, exhausting climb is *pumpy*.

- **Send.** Finish a route or boulder problem.

- **Sewing machine leg.** When a climber's leg shakes uncontrollably while standing on a small hold or in an awkward position for too long.

*(continued on next page)*

## CLIMBING SLANG *(continued from previous page)*

- **Shake out.** Taking an arm off a hold (at a suitable place on the route) so the climber can shake some blood back into it and reduce the level of lactic acid. This is sometimes referred to simply as a *shake*.

- **Sketch or sketching.** To climb in a manner that is not precise or solid. If a climber is sketching, either she's about to fall off or she's getting gripped from fear or fatigue and her technique is getting sloppy.

- **Thrutch.** Basically the same as *sketching*; however, it also may imply that the climbing is awkward.

- **Tufa.** A hold resembling a baguette, requiring the climber to use a pinch grip with one or both hands.

amount of energy possible and how to rest and recover whenever there is an opportunity. I've talked about how important your feet and your legs are, but there is a certain amount of energy spent by your arms as well. Because your arms don't have the kind of strength and stamina that your legs do, you must be very wise about preserving whatever strength you do have. Here are two great ways to save your upper body.

1.    **Hang off of straight arms whenever you're not moving.** In learning to climb, I was often told "hang off your bones" as a way to get me to straighten my arms and stop contracting muscles that didn't need to be used. The concept of hanging off your skeletal structure rather than your muscles may sound odd, but it's less taxing on your muscles. When you catch yourself gripping the holds really tightly with your arms bent, straighten them out and you'll save a lot of strength.

2.    **Rest whenever you can.** By resting I mean, while on a climb, find places that you can stop and get a little recovery. If you get up to big holds or find a position such as a stem where you can take a lot of weight off your arms, stop there for a moment or two and rest. Stemming is one of the best body positions for resting. When climbers find a rest, they usually hang their arms down and shake them around gently. This shaking out gets the lactic acid and the pumped feeling out of the arms. The term *shake* is used even to refer to a place where you can rest and shake out, as in, "If you can make it up just two more moves, there's a good shake." Finding rest positions is a talent that is just as critical as any of the movements I discuss in this chapter.

• • • • • • • • • • • • • • • • • • • • • • • • • • • • • • • • • • • • • • • • • • • • • • • • • • • • • •

**A** good climber is not only efficient in her moves, but she also knows how to use the least amount of energy possible and how to rest and recover whenever there is an opportunity.

• • • • • • • • • • • • • • • • • • • • • • • • • • • • • • • • • • • • • • • • • • • • • • • • • • • • • •

## BASIC TECHNIQUES: CRACK CLIMBING

There are many variables in how you climb a crack: it depends on the size, the direction the crack angles, how steep it is, and how consistent the width of the crack is. For this book I give the basic techniques for climbing different widths of cracks.

Simply put, you'll climb a crack by jamming your fingers, your hands, your feet, and in some cases your entire body into the crack. The easiest way to do this is to wedge them above a natural constriction in the crack and then pull or push on the constriction as you would a handhold or foothold on a face climb. When there is no constriction—that is, when the sides of the crack are parallel throughout—you will have to create a jam by *torquing* (twisting) the body part you've inserted.

I will reiterate that for all these crack techniques, what you do with your feet is most important to your success. As with face climbing, your goal is to keep your weight on your feet and let your legs do most of the work.

### Types of jamming you'll need to learn

### Finger lock

If the crack is narrow enough and there are irregular constrictions in it, you can put your fingers in above where the crack narrows down and then slide them down until they *lock* where the crack constricts. For most *finger locks*, you'll insert your fingers with the hand positioned *thumbs down* (with the thumb pointing down) in the crack. Your index finger is therefore on the bottom with the other fingers stacked on top of it; your thumb may be resting inside the crack, just below your index finger. This is by far the most common way to use a finger crack. If the crack is parallel sided, you may have to create your own locking by twisting (or *camming*) your fingers in the crack. You may also find

Climber using both a **thumbs-up** and a **thumbs-down** finger lock.

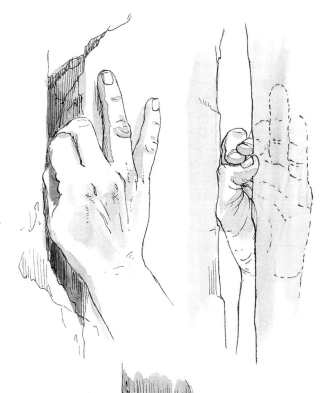

that in very small cracks, only your pinkie finger fits in. In this case, the thumb is up and you'll stack your other fingers on the pinkie to create more of a jam.

The challenge of thin, finger-size cracks is how to use your feet, because it will be difficult to get toe jams in such a narrow crack. Usually, you will need to find holds on the face for your feet; stemming holds are ideal. If the edges of the crack are offset, you may be able to press one foot against the edge that is raised while leaning off to the side to create pressure on that foot (a kind of variation on the lie back technique explained earlier in this chapter). You can also look for places where the edges of the crack flare outwards; you can get a kind of smearing toe jam in these flares. If you find absolutely nothing you can use besides the crack, by all means try wedging the outside edge of your shoe in the crack. It just may offer enough purchase to get a little higher on the climb and possibly onto better footholds.

## Finger stacking

If the crack is perfectly parallel and too wide to get a secure finger lock but too narrow to accept your whole hand, you may need this advanced technique. *Finger stacking* (also called a *thumb cam* or *ring jam*) requires using the thumb with the fingers stacked on top of it and then torquing or camming the whole unit to jam it in the crack. With your thumb pointing up, you'll insert it into the crack and push the pad against one side of the crack. With the index finger on top of your thumb right at its first joint, you'll then cram the other fingers on top of them. Then you'll twist downward on it with the goal of wedging the index finger between the top of the thumb and the side of the crack. This is probably one of the hardest jams to master, so don't get discouraged if it takes some time to get it. It'll also require that you really be on your feet, as these types of jams are pretty insecure—even when you've mastered the technique.

**Top:** Whether called a **finger stack**, **thumb cam**, or **ring jam**, this size of crack is difficult to master. **Above:** Hand jam.

# Hand jam

*Hand jamming* is by far the most secure crack climbing technique. You'll begin by inserting your hand, with the fingers pointing straight in, as far as it takes to get the heel of your hand into the crack. You'll want to make sure the meaty part of the base of your thumb joint is in the crack. Whether you slot your hand with the thumb facing up or down depends entirely on the crack. There are no rules for straight-up cracks; mostly trial and error and experience help you recognize what to use. However, with slanting hand cracks, there is a rule to follow, a rule mandated by what's physically possible and practical. If the crack diagonals to the right, your right hand will lead, thumbs-down, and your left hand will shuffle behind it, thumbs up. You will also probably keep your right foot on the face, with your left foot working the crack. Of course, a left-leaning crack requires the opposite.

Once you've learned how to do them, **hand jams** are the most secure of the jamming techniques. Leavenworth, Washington.

If I had to make a generalization, I'd say most of the time thumbs-up jams are the best choice because they feel very solid even as you climb up on them. You can't really get them very high above your head but, as I mentioned above for the feet, you're better off making small movements anyway. If you do reach high above your head and you're quite extended, you may find that a thumbs-down jam is best because you can get that critical base-of-the-thumb part of your hand into the crack in this position. However, be aware that, as you move up on a thumbs-down jam, it becomes less secure.

Once your hand is in the crack, you will flex your whole hand, focusing on squeezing your thumb in, toward your palm. The idea is to expand your hand to fit the crack. This expansion is achieved by cupping the palm and flexing hard with the thumb muscle to make that meaty part of the thumb even fatter.

I must tell you that hand cracks can be brutally abrasive to the skin, which is why many climbers tape their hands for this type of climbing. (I cover taping in chapter 8.) Besides that precaution, however, you can also minimize this brutality by taking time to set your jams carefully and then not fidgeting around with them too much. Just set them, trust them, and let your feet and your legs do most of the work.

Hand-size cracks usually offer very solid toe and foot jams, which allow you to really stand on your feet. To use a toe jam, you'll first turn your foot sideways so the instep is facing upward (your knee will be bent and out to the side to do this movement); then you'll slot your toe into the crack. As with jamming your fingers or your hands, it helps to jam your foot above a place where the crack narrows down, if possible. Once in the crack, you will twist your foot and stand up on it, trying to orient the sole of your foot back to its normal standing position. Your knee will come back into its normal alignment as you stand up.

As I said above, you'll want to take small steps. You can shuffle your feet—that is, have one foot that is always higher—or you can alternate—walking your feet up the crack. There are no set rules about this; it will depend on the crack and what feels better. Whatever you do, you'll follow the same advice as for face climbing: keep your heels below your toes or, at most, level with your toes.

## Fist jam

If the crack is too wide for a hand jam, you'll need to use a *fist jam*. Fortunately, if you don't seek them out, you won't run into too many cracks requiring this type of jamming. My first words of advice are to look thoroughly for any natural constrictions where you might be able to make use of your fist as a wedge.

For actual fist jamming, where the crack is more or less parallel sided, you'll need to get creative. Because there are various sizes of *fist cracks* (cracks that require the use of a fist jam), you'll need to experiment with different fist configurations. Make a normal fist jam by clenching your hand into a fist with the thumb on the outside, wrapped over the other fingers. To make it a little bigger, move the thumb higher so that it wraps over the index finger near where it meets the big joint where the finger and hand meet. In this position, really clench your fingers into your palm and you can see the fist widen. For narrower fist cracks you'll need to experiment with putting your thumb inside your fist or by putting your fist in the crack with your thumb up and then rotating your hand. In general, you'll use a fist jam with your palms facing down; however, you'll need to try some twisting, and even some palms up if that is what's working.

Luckily, the feet work well in a crack of this width; you'll be able to get the entire forefoot into the crack. If you have a small, average-size woman's foot, you'll probably need to torque the foot in the crack to make an effective jam or you may even need to wedge the whole foot at a slight angle to get a tight heel-toe wedge between the sides of the crack. Remind yourself to let your feet do most of the work to ease the discomfort and insecurity of your fist jams.

## Off-width

Once the crack size gets too big for fist jams but is still too small to accommodate your entire body, it is deemed an off-size crack or simply an *off-width*. This is without a doubt the most difficult, and to some the most disagreeable, size of crack to climb. I must admit that even when I was crack climbing a lot, I always felt intimidated by off-widths. It didn't help that each one I climbed felt incredibly exhausting and the furthest thing from graceful. Although I was able to get up most of them, I always found it to be an exercise in thrashing and struggling, with every muscle in my body flexed to capacity. Not many climbers I know would disagree with my representation of what it's like to climb cracks this size, and so the art of off-width climbing has few adherents. Should you find yourself faced with an off-width, I'll give you what few tips I have that might make your attempt more successful.

I first must emphasize the importance of your foot placements for off-width climbing. I've said it so many times before, but with off-width climbing, it is beyond important; it's the only way you can make upward progress. You will have only one leg in the crack, as well as one arm, and you'll be facing sideways to the crack. The other leg and the rest of your body will be somewhere between in and completely out of the crack. You may use your inside leg to brace the knee or leg between the sides of the crack, known as a *knee bar* or *leg bar*. Or, at times, the foot that is in the crack will be able to heel-toe, that is, your toes will be pushing down on one side of the crack while your heel is pressed against the other side of the crack. However, this is not

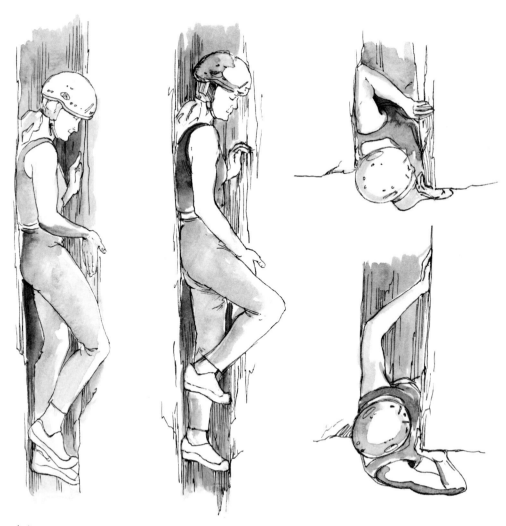

Off-width technique.

the foot that is really doing the work of pushing you up the climb. It is more for support and to take some of the strain of the whole mission. Your other leg will also be doing a heel-toe but on the outside of the crack. In lucky circumstances, there may even be footholds on the edge of the crack to use for the outside foot. You'll slowly inch your way up with small (very small) movements.

Depending on the size of the off-width, your hands and arms will be doing different things. Their most important job, however, will be to hold your body in place so that you can push yourself up with the outside leg. If you try to use your arms for anything but this (say, for hauling the rest of you up), you will waste tremendous amounts of energy. The classic position for the hands and arms is with the inside arm at chest level, creating an *arm bar* (one palm pressing on the forward wall and the upper arm and elbow pressing against the back wall). The outside hand grasps the edge of the crack with the palm facing away from you, thumbs down at about chin level. This is a game of opposition, like so many moves in climbing. You'll need to press very hard against the sides of the crack while you reset your feet. Then let the legs do their pushing task, and repeat until the end.

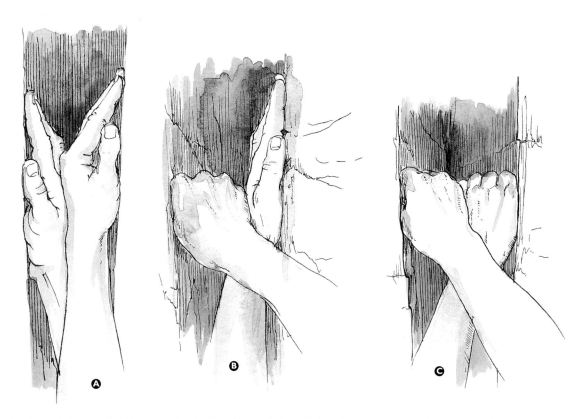

Another technique to off-width cracks is **handstacking**. Figures A, B, and C show different ways of stacking your hands/fists. Which one you use will depend on the size of the crack. **(A)** Both hands jamming against each other for smaller off-width sizes. **(B)** A fist jammed against the other hand for small-to-average size off-widths. **(C)** Fist stacked against fist for slightly bigger sizes.

I will tell you of another trick I learned later in my crack climbing career. It is a technique called *Leavittation* (named after Randy Leavitt, the climber who devised the technique). It entails using a move called *hand stacking*. The principle of setting your feet is the same as in classic off-width style: you'll get nowhere with Leavittation if you don't have good, solid foot placements or knee jams. Hand stacking is done by jamming your hands against one another, while they are jammed against the sides of the crack. The most bomber way to stack is to have your palms facing away from each other and cupped as they would be in a typical hand jam. The next best method is to have one hand jamming with its palm facing the side of the crack against the other hand, which is making a fist. Stacking is remarkably solid. However, by the same token, it has an unfortunate flaw: you cannot let go with either hand to get a higher stack unless your feet are incredibly well situated. Otherwise, when you release one hand, you have no support whatsoever and you'll probably fall. That said, if there are good feet to be found—an edge here or there on the inner walls of the crack or some sort of knee bar with your leg straight in and bent—go for it. It's certainly a more enjoyable way to climb off-width cracks.

> **U**sing your feet is universally regarded as the key to moving well.

## Chimney

The next size after an off-width, a *chimney* is a crack that is so wide that your entire body fits inside the crack while you're climbing. This can be a mixed blessing because it allows you to use both sides of the crack in many combinations of pushing and pulling. It can be quite secure; however, because a chimney may be 2 to 4 feet wide, there is no piece of protection that is large enough to allow the leader to protect herself in case of a fall. That's not usually a great problem, because it's very hard to fall out of a chimney crack.

One of the best ways to climb a chimney is to push your back against one of the walls of the chimney while your feet are pushing against the opposite wall. When you need to move upward, you'll put one foot underneath your backside while keeping the other foot on the opposite (facing) wall. As your feet are opposing each other, you'll straighten your legs and push your body upwards. Then you'll alternate by putting the other foot under your bum and repeating the sequence. All the while, to aid in getting the weight off your feet to move them up, you'll use your hands to help brace yourself in position by palming and pushing against both walls. Keep repeating the movements until you get to the top. You can also stem a chimney: keep one hand and one foot on one side of the chimney while the other hand and foot press against the opposite wall.

Describing climbing moves with words on paper is a bit like trying to explain riding a bike to someone who's never done it before. She won't really "get it" until she gets on the bike and feels the sensation of finding her balance while coordinating the pedal strokes and steering. So don't

**Left:** In chimney cracks, your whole body is inside the crack. Use your hands, feet, and even your backside to push against the sides of the cracks to make upward movement. **Above:** Climbing a chimney.

worry if some of these concepts seem bewildering at first; you'll understand much more once you get out and try it. At that point, you might want to reread some of this chapter—it will make more sense then.

The key in this chapter for you to remember during your first climbing experience is how important your feet are. If you can focus on footwork and manage to stand on your feet and push with your legs, you will excel in this sport. It sounds simple, doesn't it? And really, it is. It just requires that you are mentally prepared to defy the instincts that would have you overgrip the handholds or pull yourself with your arms. Fortunately, you will likely get some friendly reminders to "use your feet!" from your instructor, as well. It's the one tip that is universally regarded as the key to moving well.

# Chapter 6

# MAKING PROGRESS

In working with women in my clinics, I've discovered that the common desire that bonds all of them is the desire to improve. Whether they just began a month ago or they have been climbing for two years, they have all fallen in love with this sport and want to be better at it. But it isn't just the women who take clinics who are striving to improve; it's nearly *all* climbers I've ever met. For some reason that is still a mystery to me, climbers have an incredibly strong desire to improve their climbing. Maybe it's because climbs are graded, and so there is a fairly clear-cut and constant metric for judging one's progress. Perhaps there is something about climbing that draws out the obsessive-compulsive side in otherwise normal people. Whatever it is, I almost guarantee that if you get into climbing, you too will be on the quest to improve.

In this chapter, I offer suggestions that I know will improve your climbing by increasing your confidence, relaxing your mind, and smoothing out your physical movements. I start with some exercises that will help you improve both your mental and your physical prowess. These are fun, climbing exercises that teach you things about your climbing, whether you're a beginner or a more advanced climber. I use these exercises in my clinics with great success for climbers of all abilities. Following the exercises, I explain specific movement techniques for more advanced climbs, give you advice on how to read a route (plan your moves), and cover more thoroughly how to be a competent belayer. Last, I delve into the mental and psychological aspects of the sport of climbing.

**W**arming up is a time to learn about your climbing and to practice things you want to improve.

## WARM-UP EXERCISES

I can't emphasize enough the importance of warming up for climbing. Warming up is a time to learn about your climbing and to practice things you want to improve. Because you will (or should) always be on climbs that are well within your abilities, when you're warming up is the ideal opportunity to practice things that you want to become second nature. Many people do their warm-up in a cursory manner; they know they should warm up, but they find it a chore and just want to get it over with as soon as possible. I take a different approach to warming up.

When the climbing gets harder, there are quite a few things that you need to be able to do naturally, without thinking: being precise in your footwork, breathing, and staying relaxed and focused. However, these things do *not* come naturally; instead, they must be practiced until they are part of your subconscious. Use the following focusing exercises to fix this information in your brain. I guarantee that if you do these exercises *every time* you warm up, your climbing will improve dramatically.

### Exercise 1: Breathing

On your warm-up route, focus on your breathing. You should concentrate on taking deep, relaxed, even breaths. You may even want to exaggerate your breathing by creating an audible blowing out sound as you exhale. Your concentration on your breathing should be so intense that you don't hear anything else and aren't distracted by other people around you or random thoughts about the climb. Your mind should be completely immersed in your breathing. Nearly everyone forgets to breathe when they struggle on a difficult section of a climb. Certainly, this doesn't help, but your instinct is to clench your abdomen and hold your breath. You may not even notice that you're doing this until you fall off and you find that you're panting and breathing hard trying to get oxygen back into your system. To get to the point of being very relaxed and natural in your breathing, you should do this exercise *every time* you warm up until you feel that, even on extremely difficult climbs, you're breathing without even realizing it.

### Exercise 2: Precise feet

Being precise with your feet sounds like an easy thing to do, but when the climbing gets hard, one of the first things we forget about is focusing on maintaining precise footwork. As you're warming up, focus on being very precise with your feet. Your eye should follow every foot placement until it is precisely and perfectly placed on the foothold. Again, the goal is to heighten your focus to the point of not hearing or noticing anything but your feet.

**C**limbing quietly and gracefully will bring you to an almost meditative state—if your focus is truly there.

## Exercise 3: Fluidity

Climbing fluidly and with quiet, graceful movements isn't just for experts. You can develop the ability to climb like this, but it takes training yourself to do so. If you get in the habit of climbing smoothly and quietly on your warm-up routes, you will climb this way in every situation. Focus on being quiet or silent in all your movements. Be keenly aware of any sound your feet are making as you place them on the footholds. This will help you climb more precisely with your feet. As with all of these exercises, climbing quietly and gracefully will bring you to an almost meditative state—if your focus is truly there. You should be so focused that you forget about everything else.

## Exercises for improvement

The most important result of these exercises is the ability to focus. In the intensity of a climbing situation, the brain is capable of thinking many different things in rapid succession, but most of those thoughts just get in the way. They are usually negative and detract from the task at hand. Instead, you need to switch off all distracting thoughts and concentrate on the immediate situation. Focus—the ability to be in the moment, 100 percent—is so important to success in climbing. Most of the time, the reason a climber fails to do a move or falls off at a certain point on a climb is that she has lost focus or concentration at that point.

The remaining exercises are designed to help you improve various aspects of your climbing. They're best done at an indoor climbing gym, but some of them can also be done outside. You'll need to do these on routes that are fairly easy for you. Do not attempt them on climbs that are at your limit. Most of them concern movement, body awareness, footwork, and pace. They're especially fun to do with a partner, so you can both share your experiences (and so you'll be less inclined to cheat).

- **Footwork commitment.** In this exercise, once you put your foot on a hold, you cannot move it. This will mean that you must be precise, you must have an awareness of where the best part of the hold is, and you must anticipate the move and what body position you need for that move in advance. This exercise eliminates poor footwork, such as the tapping or fidgeting of a foot once it's on a hold. It also helps develop the ability to think ahead.

- **Climb a route while looking only at your hands.** This exercise will force you to find footholds by feeling them with your feet or by your body's memory of what you had used for your hands. Then you'll stand on them, really trusting them, without benefit of knowing how big they are. You'll have to make an effort to keep your head and eyes looking upward, so you'll want to enlist the help of your partner to keep you from straying. This exercise will help you develop an awareness of the sensations under the soles of your feet.

- **Climb a route while looking only at your feet.** In this exercise, you'll be feeling around for handholds with your head down, looking at your feet. You will need to be well situated and solid on your feet while you sweep the wall above for the next handhold. You'll seek out holds that are positioned so that you remain in balance on your feet.

- **Climb blindfolded.** This is the extreme of the previous two exercises. It is the ultimate in body awareness exercises and will teach you a lot about trust, tactile sensation of both your hands and your feet, and how to climb in balance. You won't be able to rely on your sight to find sequences or holds, so you'll have to trust your body's awareness and its ability to remain in balance.

- **Three- to five-second locks.** In this exercise, you'll reach up to a handhold and position your hand just above the hold as it would be in the moment before you grab it. Then, without touching the hold at all, you'll keep your hand in this position for a count of three (or more) seconds before you actually grab the hold. This exercise is an excellent way to learn about body position. You won't be able to just lunge, out of balance, to the next hold. This exercise forces you to be in a good, in-balance body position, really standing on your feet; you simply won't be able to hold the position for the required three seconds if you're not. It's super fun because it teaches you so much about how you normally climb. Nearly everyone I've ever watched do this exercise has come away with a whole new perspective on how they move in climbing.

- **Climb in slow motion.** This exercise is a little bit like the three-second lock in that it requires you to be in balance because it is difficult to not move rapidly when you aren't in balance. It will also help you learn to be fluid and quiet in your climbing. For those who only know how to rush up a route, it teaches your body to climb at a different pace. This can be important on, for example, very tenuous, technical slab climbs.

- **Speed climb a route.** This exercise needs to be done on an easy route with mostly full-hand-size holds, which should be easy to find at an indoor gym. Speed climbing is exactly as it sounds: climbing as fast as you can without care or concern about proper technique. It seems contrary to everything I've tried to impart in this chapter and the previous chapters, but this exercise is a good one for working on pace. We all tend to climb at the same pace, but there are times when we need to change the tempo; unless you've practiced climbing faster or slower than your normal pace, you won't find it easy to shift your rhythm.

Of the challenges of climbing, Rebecca Rusch says: "Climbing is not easy. It is a battle at times. It is sometimes the most frustrating, frightful, challenging thing I do. 'Why am I doing this?' is one of the statements I have been known to utter, or maybe shout. On the other hand, climbing is also the most rewarding, confidence-boosting, invigorating thing I do. Some of my best memories are of standing on top of a summit with a good friend, yodeling to celebrate our hard-earned ascent.

> "**C**limbing is the one thing I have found that continues to test me emotionally, physically, and intellectually. It can be a battle or a beautiful dance. I will never master it but will keep trying."
>
> —Rebecca Rusch, climbing instructor

"Without the struggle, sweating or fear, the reward wouldn't be as great. Climbing is the one thing I have found that continues to test me emotionally, physically, and intellectually. It can be a battle or a beautiful dance. I will never master it but will keep trying."

## USING SPECIFIC HOLDS AND TECHNIQUES

In addition to the movements I covered in chapter 5, there are several more advanced techniques that you should begin to dabble with. They are techniques that give you a distinct advantage in certain situations. Quite frankly, if you're reading this section and you're still at the beginner level, you may have a hard time executing or understanding some of these moves—and you won't need them just yet. It's when you start pushing yourself to the next level and start cracking into some harder grades that you'll really need to start experimenting with these techniques. I've decided to include them in this book because I was taught "the expert's secrets" as a beginner and it made a huge difference in my progress. Just being aware that certain moves existed—even if I couldn't execute them perfectly—allowed me to start experimenting early on, and I mastered them much more quickly than someone of my experience level normally did.

For each movement, I include the type of terrain or the situation you might encounter that would call for it.

### Outside edging

*Outside edging* is particularly useful on steeper (vertical to overhanging) climbs. I often tell people this is a way to "be taller," because it gives you extra reach. The outside edge of your shoe is used instead of the inside edge where your big toe is. You'll still want to stand primarily on your toes, but in this case your weight will be over the pinkie and the second-to-last toe. When you stand on your outside edge, your entire body will be facing sideways to the wall you're climbing on. This allows one side of your body to be quite close to the wall, which is critical on overhanging routes. Often when using the outside edge—when the plane of your body is really perpendicular to the wall—your other foot is just extended and resting against the wall, not on any particular hold. It is there simply for balance, because your weight will be entirely on the foot that is outside edging.

Using the outside edge of your foot in **outside edging** (below), and closeup in another situation (right). **Bottom:** Using a drop knee.

Pushing with the outside edge in conjunction with pulling against a handhold with the opposite hand is an ideal, balanced position. This push/pull technique is similar to the "lie back" move, which we covered in chapter 5.

## Drop knee (or back step)

The *drop knee* (or *back step*) technique is a variation of stemming and, like stemming, is useful in taking weight off the arms. The drop knee is most valuable on vertical to overhanging terrain. To get into a drop knee, you'll find a stemmed position for your feet—that is, two footholds you can push against. (Refer to chapter 5 if you need a refresher in stemming.) Then you'll rotate your body so that your hips and torso are sideways to the plane of the wall, which is accomplished by simultaneously pivoting on one of the footholds and bending and dropping one knee. That knee will be pointing in the same direction that your body is facing, and you will be pushing harder on this foot than on the other. The key to a successful drop knee lies in the hips: the inside hip should be close to the wall, and you should truly be facing sideways to the wall you're climbing on.

## Pushing yourself laterally toward the next hold

I mentioned in chapter 5 that one foot does more pushing than the other. This has to do with staying in balance as we move upward. To repeat the concept: you'll be standing and pushing with the foot that is on the opposite side of the hand that is doing the pulling (for example, the right hand pulling while pushing with the left foot). However, there are times, especially when you're standing on your outside edge, that your other foot *can* do some of the work of pushing toward the next handhold. The nonweighted foot can be used to push against a hold at knee (or even hip) level to get to a hold that is diagonally up and opposite it. That is, you'll be pushing your body laterally and diagonally up to the next handhold with the nonweighted foot. This technique works very well when you feel you don't have any more ability to push upward because the leg on which most of your body weight is resting is completely extended. To save energy, this move could be done using momentum. Think about swinging yourself up and over to the hold, with the catalyst for starting that swing originating with the laterally pushing foot.

> To be very efficient in your climbing, much of the upward movement should be generated by your hips.

### Hip position

This isn't really one specific move but a general position that is very important to making progress as the angle steepens. To be very efficient in your climbing, much of the upward movement should be generated by your hips—a concept I didn't learn until I'd been climbing for many, many years. On steep terrain, practice *leading* with your hips (making your hips the first part of your body to move up). Remember that this is your center of gravity—where it goes, you go. You'll also want to keep your hips in close to the wall on overhanging climbs because this is how you keep the force over your feet. This technique is the opposite of slab climbing, in which your hips would be away from the wall to have your center of gravity over your feet; the laws of physics are in charge here. When a handhold seems to be just out of reach, you can make yourself "taller" by moving your hips sideways and closer to the wall; you'll need to combine outside edge or back step footwork to accomplish this, as I've described earlier in this chapter.

### Flagging

*Flagging* is a technique for creating balance when the foot that you're standing on is on the same side of your body as the pulling hand (for example, the right foot is pushing and the right hand is pulling). This, of course, is a movement that will put you out of balance unless you counter it by extending the other leg far to the same side of your body as a sort of cantilever or counterbalance move. You may naturally flag without realizing how or why you got into the position. This happens when you end up trying to move one hand upward while the hand-and-foot combination you're pushing with is on the same side of your body (for example, the right hand is moving up to the next hold while the left hand and left foot are the points of contact). Typically, the leg goes

behind the one that is weighted; however, in steeper climbing you may need to use an *inside flag*, in which the leg crosses in front of the weighted foot before being extended out to the side. The inside flag keeps the hips closer to the wall.

## Rolling up to moves and climbing with straight arms

In chapter 5, I talked about hanging off straight arms when you aren't moving. This practice can also be applied sometimes to *making* moves, especially on steeper terrain. Whenever possible, you want to avoid bending your arms. Now this may sound absurd: don't we need to bend our arms as our bodies move upward? The answer is no, not always. If you're using good technique, your legs—as I have stated countless times—are pushing your body upward toward the next holds. You can accommodate the height you gain with your arms by bending them *or* by rolling up to the next holds. The *rolling* of this move is really just your torso twisting to the right or to the left so you're not facing the wall straight on. This twisting allows you to gain height on your handhold without much bending of your arm. It should be done with fluidity and momentum whenever possible. Sometimes you can even make upward progress without bending your arms at all. This is especially true when you can pull outward on your handhold, not just downward. By pushing with the feet positioned high relative to the handhold, you can pull out on the hold while pushing with your feet to create a dynamic arcing movement upward.

## Cross-through moves

Sometimes a route or a boulder problem traverses rather than goes straight up. Usually when traversing sections of climbs, you'll need to use a *cross-through move*, in which you'll cross one arm over (or under) the other to reach the next hold in the traverse. When you cross through to the

**Top:** With weight on your left foot, the right leg "flags" to the left to keep the body in balance. **Above:** Climb with **straight arms** whenever possible.

next handhold in the traverse, it is very important that you work your feet in concert with the new position of your hands. Otherwise, you'll experience that out-of-balance feeling known as the barn-door effect. Your feet should move in the same direction and should be placed on a foothold that will get your mass right under the "new" handhold. People also create the barn-door effect by letting go of the "old" handhold once they get their "new" handhold but before they have repositioned their feet. You must *not* release the "old" handhold until you've gotten your feet right underneath the new handhold. If the cross-through move was a big one, you may need to walk your feet by taking several baby steps to get them established under the new handhold.

## Heel hooking

Using your heel in climbing footwork is pretty rare, although there are some times when it's the best choice. *Heel hooking* is exactly as it sounds: you hook

A classic **cross-through** move.

the back of your heel on a hold instead of pressing on it with your toes. This technique is employed most often when trying to negotiate the point where the horizontal plane of a roof turns back to vertical (known as the *lip transition*) of a horizontal section (a *roof*) or on outside corners

(*âretes*). You'll hook your heel over the lip of a roof on a hold and then pull with that foot until you can get your body weight over the foot, which usually isn't until most of your torso gets above the lip. At that point, you'll rock your weight over the heel and then turn the heel hook into the normal toe-on position. Heel hooks are often positioned very high, around waist or even chest height, and are pulled with as opposed to being pushed on, as most other foot placements are. Using a heel hook is somewhat like having a third arm; in the right situations, it can take over for much of the pulling by the arms.

**Heel-hooking** is a rare foot placement, but it's very effective in the right situation. Eau de Colonne, Russan, France.

## READING ROUTES

Climbing movement, unlike the repetitive movement in running or cycling, is not something that can be done with your brain switched off. A climbing route presents you with a series of holds that you'll use with both your hands and your feet in a certain sequence. If it's a very easy route, with lots of big holds, it won't take much thought; you'll climb it as you would a ladder—by simply grabbing whatever comes next. However, once you get past the beginner-style routes that have holds everywhere, climbing will require more creative thinking and creative moving. If you're learning in a gym, the handholds and footholds will be very obvious, even from the ground looking up at the route. Outside on natural rock, however, the holds will be less obvious until you are actually on the route.

Indoors or out, here are the steps you should take *before* every climb.

- **Start by looking at the entire route in a general way.** Note the starting holds, the overall line of the route, and where it ends. If you're outside, use guidebook topo drawings to find points of reference, such as a tree, a big boulder at the base, a prominent leaning crack line, or an obvious feature such as an inside corner or an ârete.

- **As you look up the route, try to find a hold that *must be* taken with a certain hand.** This is often more evident on indoor routes. Once you find the obligatory handhold, reverse the moves downward from that point to help you figure out the proper sequence of moves. Likewise, you can continue with the sequence above that point. Here's an example: You can see that you must have your right hand on hold Y because the next hold (hold Z) is up and to the left; you can tell it will be impossible to cross over to hold Z if you ended up with your left hand on hold Y. With this information, you figure out that to get your right hand on hold Y, you must have your left hand on the previous hold (hold X)—and so on down the line of the route, alternating left hand, right hand. In this study of the route, you may also see holds that appear big enough to match both hands on. Just be certain that you remember what hand needs to lead off any hold you've matched on.

- **Make a note of all of the footholds that you can see.** For gym routes, determine in advance whether a hold is meant to be only a foothold. I often see people in the gym start using what the course setter intended to be just footholds. These are usually much smaller than the holds that are intended for both hands and feet, so they make the route much harder than it actually is.

- **Look for possible rest positions.** You want to climb the route in sections, from rest position to rest position. Mentally, it's less intimidating to think of it this way instead of as one big, nonstop climb from the bottom to the top. Look for inside corners where you can get a stem, ledges or big holds where you can stand comfortably, places that become lower angle so you need your hands only for balance. All of these offer resting potential.

- **Look for sections where you don't want to stop or hesitate.** If there's a bulge, a roof, or another steep section, you'll want to move through it as quickly as possible. In overhanging sections, you can't afford to hang out there for too long; it will only sap your strength if you do. Rest up before the section and after it, if you can, but once you get there, don't hesitate.

- Once you've worked out a sequence from start to finish, **have a little run-through in your mind and even physically mime the moves in the air** as you look at the route again before starting up. Your muscles will actually remember what your mind has imagined, especially if you add the simulated movement.

- **Once you're on the route, be flexible with the sequence you've worked out.** Even though you may have figured out something from the ground that you were sure was right, be prepared to change it if the move you're attempting doesn't seem feasible or if you realize you made a mistake. This is especially true if the move seems far harder than the rest of the moves you've done or if it seems to be far more difficult than the overall grade of the route would normally have.

- **Once you're on the route, follow the most traveled path.** On routes outside, the holds will be less obvious. Look for chalk and black rubber boot dust on smaller holds, which might indicate the best footholds. Opt for taking the line of least resistance, but always look ahead to make sure the path you've chosen doesn't peter out above.

## BECOMING A COMPETENT BELAYER

Belaying is your biggest responsibility as a climber. The safety of your climbing partner will depend on your belaying. This is not meant to intimidate you, but rather to stress the importance of becoming skilled, attentive, and proficient in your belaying. Although the movements of feeding the rope into or out of the belay device, all the while never letting the brake hand go from the rope, seem to be awkward at first, they will become more natural and fluid with practice. Mastering this one technique doesn't make you a competent belayer, however; there's more to good belaying than simply managing the rope through the belay device.

Tips for better belaying:

1.  Double-check your harness and knot, as well as your partner's. There would be no amount of competency in the belay that could rectify an accident caused by not being tied in correctly.

2.    If the climber you're belaying is leading, *stack* (pile) the rope so that it feeds out from the top of the pile. If you are uncoiling or laying each coiled strand into a neat pile or stack so it feeds smoothly as you belay (that is, *flaking*) a coiled rope out, be sure to hand your climber the top end of the rope to tie into. If you're using a rope bag and you're not sure which end is on top, you may need to restack the rope to be sure it will feed smoothly.

3.    For lead belaying, position yourself so that you are in a stable position, not too far from the base of the wall and in line with where the rope is running up to the climber's first piece of protection. Do not stand either too far out from the wall or too far to either side of the line of the climber. If the climber falls, you will be pulled in toward the wall; if you're off to the side, you'll get dragged over and will end up directly under the climber's line anyway.

problem: weight difference too great          problem: belayer too far from wall

problem: belayer beneath an overhang          problem: belayer releases brake hand

Various situations resulting from the belayer not being properly anchored or not in line with the climber.

"The best climbers in the world will tell you that climbing is mostly a mental game. I have repeatedly been astounded by the power of the mind in my own climbing. I've found over and over again that my greatest climbing successes were because of my mental fitness, rather than my physical fitness."

—Elena Ovchinnikova, 34, mother of two, one of the top competition climbers in the world

4. Anchor yourself appropriately. With the exception of belaying in the gym, you will need to be anchored so that you do not get pulled up when your climber falls. When belaying your climber from the ground, as you would for the first pitch of a climb, you'll probably be tied into a tree or a boulder. For belays above the ground, on multi-pitch climbs, or on routes lacking a conveniently placed tree or boulder at the base, the anchor will be set up by the leader using removable protection. Sometimes the first ascent party will fix the belay station with permanent bolts. No matter what the anchor is, you must be tied into it without much slack between your belay stance and the anchor. In the event of a fall—especially if the climber is heavier than you are or if the fall is severe enough—if you have a loop of slack between you and the anchor, you will be pulled up, dragged, and slammed into the wall until you are taut to the anchor. This is neither a pleasant experience nor a safe one. In gym climbing, particularly when the climber is top roping, the belayer is rarely anchored, because there isn't much force created in a top rope fall. For lead climbing in the gym, however, it's good practice to be anchored. Gyms usually have fixed anchors coming out of the floor that you can either tie into or clip directly into the belay loop of your harness. (See knots used for tying into anchors, chapter 4.)

5. Be sure to indicate to the climber when the belay device is rigged, the locking carabiner is locked, and you're ready to give your full attention to the task. (Remember the signals? "Belay on.") (See page 49.)

6. Once the climber begins, make sure that you keep pace with her movements and rate of ascent. The leading climber should never feel the rope tugging at her harness as she climbs nor should she have to struggle to clip the rope into her protection. You should pay out just enough rope so that she can move smoothly, but not so much that you have a loop of slack from your belay device to the wall, because this would create a longer fall if the climber came off at that moment. The top roped climber should never have a loop of slack above

her, nor should she feel as if she is being pulled up the route by the rope. The good belayer is always attentive to the movements of her climber.

7.  Make certain that you have understood what your climber has called down to you. There have been stories of miscommunication in which the climber had said "take" but the belayer thought she heard "off" (as in "off belay") and took the climber off. The climber, presuming that the belayer had taken her, leaned back on the rope but was no longer on belay, so the climber fell to the ground. Scary, huh? It underscores the importance of using the climbing signals I explained in chapter 4. And don't hesitate to call up to get clarification if you're not sure what you heard.

## UNDERSTANDING THE MENTAL SIDE OF CLIMBING

When you first start climbing, your mind will react to what it perceives as a threatening situation. When this happens and fear takes over, you'll tend to forget all you've learned about good technique and your movements will be less than precise. Your greatest mental task will be to rise above your own natural instincts and use reason and rational thought to overcome these sensations. To help you with this challenge, I've included some mental tips that I've used for years. I use these "mental tricks" almost as mantras when my mind is trying to push the panic button. By repeating the appropriate trick, my mind is forced to concentrate on that, instead of on the feelings of fear or panic. When you start feeling desperate, plug in one of my mental tricks to get your focus back where it needs to be.

### Some common mental stumbling blocks

## Fear of failure (or fear of success)

Here is a common refrain I've heard from women of all levels: "So many times when I get near the end of a route, my heart starts racing, my forearms suddenly feel like they're going to explode, and my mind starts rushing through a litany of reasons why I'm not going to make it. I usually fall off within moments. What can I do?" This is a pretty common situation: although we are teetering on the brink of success, our mind steps in and takes over with lots of chatter and negativity. It may seem that we got instantly pumped at that point. We don't know really whether it was our mind or our body that failed us. Nine times out of ten, I say it's the mind that wins out. This may sound like pop psychology, but I've seen this phenomenon in action too many times to discredit its power over the outcome of our endeavors.

It's important that you focus on the climbing and not let your mind fill with other distracting, negative thoughts. Easier said than done, you may be thinking. That's true; it *will* take some effort. You'll need to be sure you're doing the warm-up exercises I suggested above so you are breathing and climbing fluidly and precisely. I also recommend doing some creative visual-

• • • • • • • • • • • • • • • • • • • • • • • • • • • • • • • • • • • • • • • • • • • • • • • • •

**Mental tricks for fear of failure (or fear of success):**

- Create *cues* that trigger states of relaxation and control. Visualize the desired response of the cue to reinforce its effect.

- Downplay the importance of outcomes. Whenever I feel a lot of pressure to do well on a route, I remind myself that no matter what happens in the next 10 minutes, my parents will love me just as much as they always have. In fact, even if the worst thing happens and I fall off the first move, they'll still love me just as much. You can replace "parents" with husband, children, grandma, or whomever you know cares more about you than they do about the route you're about to attempt.

- Keep reminding yourself about all of the things that are truly important in the world—and in your life. Your success or failure on one route is fairly meaningless in the big picture.

• • • • • • • • • • • • • • • • • • • • • • • • • • • • • • • • • • • • • • • • • • • • • • • • •

ization exercises when you're at home relaxing. There are many sport psychology books that describe the process for getting into a physical state for visualization (see chapter 10). In your visualization, you will put yourself in highly stressful climbing situations where you really feel you're at your physical limit. Once there, you will visualize yourself as relaxed and calm, with your mind keenly focused only on your perfect footwork and the moves you're executing. I added one element to my visualization that I hadn't read about before (although I'm sure it's not original). I incorporate cues that I then use in real-life situations. In my visualizations, I see myself breathing a strong, forceful breath out, I hear the sound of it, and I experience it fully in my mind. That exhalation triggers a state of even greater focus and precision within my visualization. If I do this enough in my mind, when I exhale on a real climb I am brought back to that same mental state I imagine in my visualizations.

More than likely, you may also need to eliminate the pressure you're putting on yourself about the outcome of your climb. When you put so much emphasis on the outcome, you are unable to focus on the climbing. You lose the ability to "be in the moment" because your mind is consumed with the consequences of your success or failure. You need to get to a point of completely letting go of the outcome of the climb and just enjoy the climbing. In competition climbing, this is what really separates the champions from everyone else. Their ability to walk up to the wall with their minds empty of expectations and outcomes is the reason they succeed. Their minds are just clean, blank canvases ready to concentrate solely on the route, the holds, the

**Y**ou need to get to a point of completely letting go of the outcome of the climb and just enjoy the climbing.

Correct body position for **falling**.

moves, and the sequence. Whether it's a competition route or a route that you really want to do or feel you *should* be able to do, the pressure is the same. And the necessity to focus on the climbing rather than on the outcome is just as critical to your success.

## Fear of falling

One of the most common fears is the fear of falling. It's the most natural human reaction because we just *know*, somewhere at the cellular level, that falling isn't a good thing. However, much of this fear has to do with the fact that we don't know what's going to happen if we fall. Even after all of the explanations about how the gear, the belay, the rope, and the harness work, you're probably still not going to be too keen to fall. Nobody is. The best way to get over this fear is to learn how to fall correctly and then to practice taking falls so that you know what to expect. Of course, the falls you take on top rope will be minimal—only so far as the rope stretches (as long as your belayer has been taking up the excess slack rope as you ascend). Taking lead falls and bouldering falls are where you really need to be aware of how to fall correctly and safely.

Here are some tips on falling well.

1.    **Keep your eyes open.** It's scary at first, but you need to be able to see where you're headed. If you're falling off a boulder problem, be sure to look down at your landing as you're falling. Watching all that is happening in the fall will help you get past this fear.

**Mental tricks for fear of falling:**

- Remember what happened to you the last time you fell (or what happened to the last climber you saw fall)—absolutely nothing!

- Picture falling as a cat would fall: relaxed, poised, and ready to land on your feet.

2.   **Fall actively, not passively.** By this I mean that you don't want to just let your body go limp like a rag doll or to crumple up into the fetal position. You'll want to get your body positioned so that it's facing the wall squarely. Your legs and feet should be positioned so that they'll be the first points of contact as you hit the wall.

> **F**alling is like any new skill you want to learn; you have to practice it until you've mastered it.

3.   **Let your legs absorb the impact of the fall.** Once your feet have hit either the wall or the ground (in the case of bouldering), your knees should act as a shock absorber by bending deeply and springing back. For this reason, you don't want to be too tense or rigid with your body; a relaxed anticipatory stance while falling is the best solution.

Falling is like any new skill you want to learn; you have to practice it until you've mastered it. You will be much more comfortable with falling once you've done it successfully a few times. You can practice falling by going up a route and purposefully letting go. The safest way to do this is with an experienced belayer on the other end of the rope. Some gyms even offer clinics on falling, which is less intimidating than practicing outside.

## Lack of confidence

For years I fell off of routes because I didn't believe I could do certain moves. Once my mind said, "I'm not going to make it" or "That's too far" or "I'm going to fall if I try this move," sure enough, it was right. Your mind will always be right, so it is up to you to change what it tells you. This example differs from the first in that you may not feel stressed about the overall outcome but instead may have a resigned attitude about your lack of ability to do a certain move. This is one I personally struggled with a lot until I figured out a way to overcome it (see Mental Trick next page).

### Build your confidence by climbing with other women

The majority of women climbers I've met learned to climb from a boyfriend, husband, or other romantic interest. Most climbers are men, so it's not that surprising that they would want to share the experience with their partners. Sometimes this situation can be great: I learned to climb from my boyfriend at the time; he was amazingly patient and happened to be a great instructor. I was also lucky that he was 2 inches shorter than I was; I could imitate his moves and they worked perfectly for my size. Not all of my other experiences climbing with men were quite so reinforcing, and this is a situation that is true for many women. This is why I cannot stress to you enough the value of climbing with other women. It is amazing what we can learn from one another.

Climbing with another woman will bring out your strengths and will help you to overcome

• • • • • • • • • • • • • • • • • • • • • • • • • • • • • • • • • • • • • • • • • • • • • • • • • • • • • • •

### Mental trick for believing you can:

The solution I found to my lack of confidence sounds crazy at first, and some people even feel a bit embarrassed to try it. However, I promise, if you give it a chance, it really works! When you look up at that move that you instantly realize is impossible, take a moment to see yourself holding the next hold and then scream as loud as you can within your own brain (not out loud) "Yes!" as you launch into the move. If I have a chance just prior to screaming "Yes!" I will even do a little silent chant that goes something like this: "Yes, I can do this move; yes, I can do this move." Now you may have to override what your brain is *really* thinking, so talk insistently and loud enough to be center stage. That's also why the "Yes!" is screamed loudly; your brain simply can't ignore it and your body has no choice but to do what your brain tells it to do.

• • • • • • • • • • • • • • • • • • • • • • • • • • • • • • • • • • • • • • • • • • • • • • • • • • • • • • •

your weaknesses. It creates a healthy competitiveness, so you'll push yourself a little harder. Seeing a woman succeed on a route inspires you and makes you believe that you, too, can do it.

When a woman climbs only with men, her progress and her confidence can be diminished—not through any deliberate act but because of the physical differences between men and women. Men naturally have more upper body strength (and sometimes lack the good sense to *not* use it) and are generally taller, so they tend to give advice that has women trying to perform physical feats that are beyond them—not to mention that may be inefficient and encourage poor technique. Women can help one another find solutions because of our size and strength similarities.

According to Keleigh Asbury: "When I finally began climbing with other women, I opened up to healthy criticism and was much more receptive to being given beta, which I had never seemed to be able to use from my male friends. I started to understand the true mechanics of my body, and so did the women I was climbing with. It made me feel like a different climber and rightfully so . . . a different person."

Sometimes a psychological aspect comes into play because climbing is a pretty intense mental activity. When the climbing gets tough and fear starts creeping in, the traditional male to female dynamic of "man as protector, woman as helpless, weaker sex" (pardon the stereotypes) can come into play. This situation does nothing to empower a woman but instead reinforces dependence. You'll be a lot bolder in your climbing when your partner is a woman; it's hard to chicken out when you don't have your big, strong, ever-ready-to-take-charge-of-things husband or boyfriend there to rescue you.

# TRUE STORIES OF CLIMBING WITH THE "MAN IN YOUR LIFE" . . .

"When I first started rock climbing with my boyfriend and some male friends of his, I had no idea what technique was. None of them had bothered to introduce me to the intricacies of the 'movement' of climbing. I scrambled around on routes just having fun and thinking that getting to the top of anything without falling was my ultimate goal. It was absolutely amazing how out of touch with my body I was for so many years. (I think that I literally climbed for two years before I even realized that I had two feet attached to my ankles.) I don't want to say that it was climbing with the boys that turned me into a galloping moose, but things really turned around for me when I started climbing with more women."

—Keleigh Asbury, 30, marketing and promotions director of Boulder Rock Club, Boulder, CO

"When we first met, my husband was an avid climber and because of his enthusiasm I was excited to try it. He was patient in his teaching, but he took care of everything; I didn't learn how to do things on my own. It wasn't like he was trying to be overbearing; it's just that he enjoyed leading and letting me just relax and have fun. It was my fault, too; I just sat back and enjoyed the ride. I never felt I could lead or even go climbing without my husband. When I finally found a friend to climb with and started taking charge of my own climbing, my climbing and my confidence in myself as a climber really improved."

—Heather Abbott, 26, graduate student, Albuquerque, NM

"The first time I went climbing, I never even got to the 'climbing' part. My boyfriend had taught me how to belay and started up a climb that was way over his head. Of course, I had no clue about his level or that the route he was on was too hard for him. The next thing I knew he was flying through the air and I was catching his fall by some miracle. I never let go of the brake hand, per his most emphatic instructions, but he was so close to the ground when he fell that he grazed a tree on his way down. He wasn't seriously hurt, but I was in shock. We left immediately as he was in a lot of pain from the road rash covering most of his torso. I still can't believe I pursued climbing after that first experience."

—Christine Vukavich, 37, Madison, WI

# Chapter 7

# THE GEAR

So far in this book, I've focused on what you can expect from climbing and the techniques for safety and movement. I've covered only the equipment you would be renting for your first climbing experiences without making too many distinctions about quality or comfort. The truth is, rental gear is fine for the first few times, but like *any* rental gear, it's usually pretty thrashed and less comfortable than what you'd buy for yourself. And it can often hinder your progression in the sport. Once you're ready to leap into climbing 100 percent, you'll want to buy your own gear.

In this chapter, I talk about how to choose the right gear for the type of climbing you'll be doing, how to get the right fit with the personal gear (such as shoes and harness), and how to care for all of it. I also cover how to spot signs of damage or excessive wear that indicate it's time to retire the gear. Although you may not yet need your own rope and rack, this chapter includes information on buying a rope and also on what gear you'll eventually want to get for setting up your own top ropes and for leading.

## HARNESS

A harness is one of the most important pieces of gear you'll buy not only because it is life saving, but also because it's crucial that you'll be comfortable when you're hanging in it. Your new harness will consist of a waist belt and leg loops constructed of nylon webbing (see photo page 49).

• • • • • • • • • • • • • • • • • • • • •

**A** good harness fit is critical
to your safety and comfort.

• • • • • • • • • • • • • • • • • • • • •

The very basic versions are made simply of webbing (similar to seat belt
material) or webbing with some fleece
sewn on the inside. However, most of
the models that you would buy for
yourself have some sort of foam
padding built in. The prices range
from as low as $45 to as high as $100.

A good fit is critical to your
safety and comfort. A knowledgeable salesperson will be able to help
you decide which harnesses would be

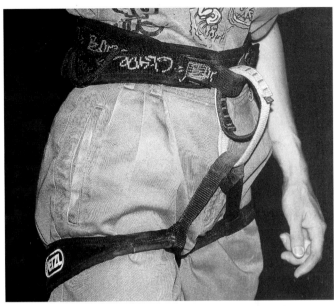

A correctly fitted harness designed for use by women.

best for your anatomy. However, don't rely entirely on a salesperson's recommendation. I suggest
trying on as many different brands and models as you can, because the fit is nearly impossible to
judge until you get it on your body. You will definitely want to "hang" in a harness before making a commitment to it. The store or gym will have a place to test harnesses this way. Have the
salesperson set you up to hang in the harness, so you can really get an idea of how it fits and how
comfortable it will be in real climbing situations. Keep in mind as well that when you're climbing, you're not hanging in the harness *all* of the time. While it's important to have the harness
be comfortable when you fall or sit in it, it's also very important to feel comfortable while you're
moving. Flexibility and maneuverability are important. The harness shouldn't dig in while you
are high stepping or twisting your body around while you're actually climbing. You should generally avoid a tight-fitting harness.

## Getting the right fit

When trying on harnesses, the biggest obstacle you'll find is that if you get the waist to fit, the leg
loops are too snug. This is because most harnesses are unisex size and do not take into account
that a woman's waist is much smaller relative to her thighs. For this reason, you may want to try
a harness specifically designed for women. Nearly every harness manufacturer has at least one
"women's" model. These harnesses are designed to fit a woman's proportions: the waist belt is
smaller, the leg loops are larger, and the rise is a bit longer compared to other models. Some of
the women's harnesses also have an adjustable rise, which is key if you're exceptionally long or
short in the rise. You may also be directed to a harness with adjustable leg loops; I don't recommend this style unless you're going to be using the harness for ice climbing or mountaineering

where you might be wearing extra clothing under the harness. In my mind, the adjustable loops are just a quick and easy way for the salesperson fitting the harness to achieve the right fit without having to spend the time trying you in several models. If you're buying a harness to be used solely for rock climbing, adjustable leg loops simply are not as comfortable, they can catch on things, and they add more weight and bulk. You should be able to get a harness that fits *your* body without having to resort to adjustable leg loops.

Here are some considerations to help you determine whether the harness fits.

- The waist belt should be snug, but not tight, at the smallest part of your waist.

- The harness should not feel as if it's pulling down in front (where the belay loop is), causing the waist belt to gap out in front or to be pulled lower than the position of the belt on the rest of your waist. If this does happen, the harness is probably too short in the rise.

- If, while sitting suspended, the waist belt rides up to your rib cage, it is either too big or too long in the rise.

- The leg loops fit correctly if you can readily fit your hand between your thigh and the webbing of the leg loops.

- While you're standing, the leg loops should rest just below the break where your thigh and your hip meet. If they're hanging much lower than this, then the harness is too long in the rise or too big overall. If the leg loops are are riding up toward your bum, the harness is probably too short in the rise or simply too small overall.

## Caring for your harness

Harnesses are constructed primarily of nylon webbing and, like ropes, will suffer the most aging if exposed for too long to UV rays. It's fine to leave the harness in your climbing pack or other bag in the back of your car, but don't leave it for any extended period in direct sunlight.

To make your harness last as long as possible, be aware of abrasion points. The most common place that a harness wears quickly is the tie-in point. This is because you continually thread and pull out the rope from this fairly small opening. The ends of all used ropes have sharp, hardened edges where the hot cut nylon has cracked; these edges abrade on the inside webbing of the tie-in loops. In itself, this abrasion would only slowly wear the tie-in point out; however, most climbers do not take care in how they pull the rope out when they've finished climbing; once untied, they usually pull the rope out as rapidly as they can. The friction that is created by the sheath of the rope on the webbing as it whips out, coupled with those sharp edges of the end of the rope, will quickly wear right through the nylon protecting the tie-in point. So pull the rope out slowly and gently for the longest life of your harness.

A properly fitting harness will last many years, but be on the lookout for signs that it needs to be retired.

- Broken stitching.

- Places on the webbing that are no longer uniform in appearance. Watch for fuzziness, broken yarns, knobby, small bumps, or any other deformation.

- Evidence that friction has worn completely through the webbing on the tie-in point.

## CHALK BAG

When you climb, your hands perspire, which reduces your feeling of security on the handholds. Climbers carry a *chalk bag* filled with carbonate of magnesium (gymnast's chalk) to dip their hands into to help alleviate that damp, sweaty feeling and to increase the friction they feel between their fingers and the handhold. Chalk is typically available in a small block and costs about $2.50. One block of chalk will normally last 8 to 12 climbing days, depending on how dependent you become on it or how hot it is. You carry the chalk with you in a small fleece-lined pouch as you climb.

Tie the bag around your waist with a piece of webbing or a thin cord. As you climb, the chalk bag sits in back, although it can slide around to either side of your body on its belt when needed. Chalk bags come in many shapes, sizes, and fabric patterns to suit your taste; it's one of the few fashion statements you can make in climbing, so have fun with it. Chalk bags cost from $16 to $20.

Your **chalk bag** is one of the few pieces of gear that can also be a fashion statement.

## DID YOU DOUBLE BACK YOUR BUCKLE?

Once you've stepped into your climbing harness, you'll need to secure the waist belt by threading the buckle and then doubling it back on itself. This is called (appropriately) *doubling back* your harness, and it's one of those often repeated safety warnings. You should make it a habit to double-check your own and your partner's harness each time you climb. The buckle on the harness is *not* safe unless it has been doubled back. Note: as mentioned in chapter 4, if you get one of the Petzl models, the harness buckle always remains threaded in the doubled-back and safe position, so you need only to pull the tail end of the belt to make it snug around your waist.

A good all-around shoe will work well on many types of climbs.

## SHOES

Climbing shoes are the one piece of gear that you will always be wearing when you're climbing. They are also the most painful and difficult to get used to of all of the pieces of gear you will wear. This is because you're not used to wearing *any* shoes that tight; however, you will quickly get used to the sensation of the correct fit of your climbing shoes. They are made with a snug-fitting leather upper and smooth, soft rubber soles; they lace up, have straps with Velcro closures, or simply slip on (with some serious tugging). The rubber on the soles and sides (*rands*) is very *sticky* (having a high friction coefficient) compared to other rubber compounds on shoes, which allows you to use very small footholds or even to adhere with friction where there are no holds.

Most climbers wear their shoes without socks. I know it sounds a bit crude, but you'll appreciate the increased sensitivity it affords. I recommend trying the shoes on without socks. The shops are quite used to this, so you needn't be worried about how they'll react.

Because climbing shoes aren't cheap (prices range from $90 to $150), you'll want to make sure you get the right fit. This is the hard part: when you first try them, you will be inclined to buy shoes that are too big. I'd say that 8 out of 10 people who stay with the sport regret their first climbing shoe purchase because they bought shoes that were too big. At the time they bought the shoes, however, they were convinced that they were way too tight. But the shoes stretched and began to loosen up with use and, possibly more significantly, the climbers' feet got used to the shoes. You actually develop calluses on your feet to be able to stand to wear your shoes properly tight. But most importantly, when you're actually climbing (and you'll have to trust me on this), you won't notice the discomfort. Believe me, you'll appreciate this advice later on when you're able to stand on very small footholds with confidence.

Here are my fit guidelines: Climbing shoes are meant to fit tightly so that there are no gaps (or *dead space*) between your foot and the inside of the shoe. If you get into them easily and they don't hurt at all, they're way too big. If they're mildly uncomfortable, they're probably still too big. You should have some discomfort but not so much acute pain that you cannot stand in the shoes for five minutes or more in the store. Your toes should be right up against the end of the shoe, possibly bunched up a little, but they shouldn't be forming a fist at the end of your foot. The most important area to make certain is snug is the front portion (from the arch forward) of the shoe. Dead space in the heel is acceptable; however, the heel shouldn't slip off when pulled. I mention this because many women have narrow heels and it's difficult to find a snug fit in this area. Truthfully, I have never owned a pair of climbing shoes that didn't have a little bagginess in the heel, but it was never a hindrance because the shoes fit so well everywhere else. You should remember that 99 percent of your climbing involves using the shoe right under your toes, which makes the design and fit of the shoe at the front the most important concern.

Because it isn't likely that you have become a specialist in any one discipline of climbing yet, for your first climbing shoe you will want to choose a model that will work well for several types of climbing—what we call an *all-around shoe*. The construction of a shoe correlates to the type of climbing for which it was designed. Following is a very broad overview of shoe types and the type of climbing for which they were designed.

## Board-lasted shoes

Board-lasted climbing shoes are designed to be quite stiff under the front of the foot; your foot will sit quite flat inside the shoe or boot. If you've never worn a climbing shoe before, your toe, foot, and ankle muscles will not be very developed. For this reason, many beginners will choose a board-lasted shoe to give them some stiffness and rigidity under their feet.

This stiffness makes board-lasted shoes more comfortable for climbing all day on slabby to vertical climbs, which will suit you if you're learning to climb in an outdoor setting. A disadvantage of board-lasted shoes is that you won't have a great deal of sensitivity under your toes, so you won't be able to "feel" the details of the footholds you choose to stand on. These types of shoes and boots are best suited to multi-pitch, traditional climbing with an emphasis on crack climbing, and small edge face climbing.

## Slip-lasted shoes

Slip-lasted shoes do what board lasted shoes cannot. You'll have the sensitivity under your toes, but the sacrifice is that you will have less support for the muscles of your foot. Slip-lasted shoes may be made either with no midsole, which makes them very soft under the foot, or with a midsole at the front of the shoe that will add some stiffness to the feel.

Apart from the construction differences, slip-lasted shoes will have a very different fit. Most are built with a *reverse camber*, which is sometimes called a *toe down* position. When you are climbing on steep terrain, you often need to "grab" holds with your toes and feet. To achieve this, the entire sole of the shoe needs to be slightly curved, a subtle imitation of the way your hand would curl around a hold as you grabbed it. Because your toes are pointing slightly downward inside the shoe, when you are edging on small holds, all of your body weight will be focused toward your big toe. This characteristic makes slip-lasted shoes great performing shoes, but you do miss out on comfort when you have to wear them for a long period of time. For this reason, I wouldn't recommend a radically down-turned, slip-lasted shoe for climbing long multi-pitch slab routes, but you will love them indoors and on steeper climbs.

In general, slip-lasted shoes with a moderately stiff midsole will be best suited to single- or multi-pitch trad or sport routes, moderate crack climbs, and face climbs, whereas those with thin or no midsoles will be best for steep overhanging climbing, shorter length face climbing, indoor gym climbing, and bouldering.

The salesperson in the store can be a great source of information about specific models—or sometimes, quite the opposite. Be aware that salespeople may have personal shoe preferences based on their own climbing styles. If you go into the store with the following points in mind, it should help you to narrow your search.

- Like harnesses, you should try many different brands and models to find the ones that fit the shape of your foot. The fit is the most important thing to get right.

- There are many specialized shoes available; however, at this stage, you're looking for a good all-around shoe—not a highly specialized model.

- Buy a brand that has a good reputation for quality and durability. On all shoes, the sole is the first thing that usually wears out—long before the uppers. However, climbing shoes can be resoled (often more than once) *if* the uppers and rands are still in good condition. Resoling costs about $30 to $35, so it's worth it to spend a little extra on your initial purchase to ensure that the shoe lasts long enough to resole. Don't hesitate to ask about the reputation of the different brands or where the shoes are made. Generally speaking, shoes made in Europe have the best reputation for quality of materials, construction, and overall finish.

Most climbing shoes are not gender specific, which generally isn't an obstacle to fitting. In fact, only one company makes a climbing shoe targeted toward women. Truthfully, I don't think that a single shoe designed for women is the answer, because just like men's feet, ours also vary greatly in shape and proportion. I have tried the "women's" climbing shoe, but the fit of this shoe didn't work for my foot; however, I have always gotten a perfect fit in many unisex models. *The design and shape is more important than gender-specific marketing hype.* More important to be aware of is the fact that your foot is a lot smaller than a man's, and in smaller sizes of *any* model the shoe will be more rigid than it will be in a larger size. Therefore, a shoe that is marketed as a "stiff" shoe (good for edging on small holds) will be ultra-stiff in smaller sizes. The same applies at the other end of the spectrum: a supple shoe (better for smearing, overhanging climbing, or climbing indoors) will be more rigid on a smaller foot and should not be ruled out. Keep in mind that these categories of stiff or supple are created by the manufacturer based on an average male-size shoe. Additionally, a stiff shoe in smaller sizes and worn by a lighter person will not soften up or break in as readily.

Liz Hunt, climber and climbing buyer for A-16 outdoor stores, confirms: "Proper fit is essential when it comes to climbing shoes and can really help your confidence in trusting your feet. Good footwork is one of the cornerstones to moving well on the rock, and having an ill-fitting shoe will do nothing but hinder you. Take your time in finding what fits you the best by trying on as many brands and models as possible. Renting shoes at your local outdoor shop or rock shoe demos is an excellent way to test-drive on real rock."

## Caring for your shoes

There isn't much involved in taking care of your shoes. You'll get the greatest performance out of the sticky rubber if you keep it fresh by cleaning it. The *spit-and-rub* method is how this is accomplished. With a bit of spit in your hand, start rubbing the sole of the shoe aggressively with the palm of your hand. You only have to do the front part of the sole. Little flakes of rubber will start coming off if you're doing it correctly. The shoe is clean when you start hearing a squeaky noise and your hand is close to dry. You should also take care to air out your shoes from time to time, especially if your feet tend to sweat a lot. If you intend to resole your shoes, you'll also want to pay attention to how the sole and the rand are wearing. Do not let your rands wear through to the leather underneath because no resole artist can help you if that happens. The best way to prevent premature rand destruction is to use good footwork. Don't drag your feet down the wall!

> "**G**ood footwork is one of the cornerstones to moving well on the rock, and having an ill-fitting shoe will do nothing but hinder you."
>
> —Liz Hunt, climbing buyer

## BELAY DEVICE

*Belay devices* are used to arrest a climber's fall. They take a great deal of the impact of the fall by the friction of the rope through the device. The device attaches to your harness belay loop with a *locking carabiner*. Some gyms or guides will supply you with a device for your first time and will teach you how to use that device. You'll ultimately be buying your own, so here's what's available and the pros and cons of each type. (If you'll be doing a lot of climbing at a gym, be aware that some gyms allow *only* certain types of belay devices. Find out in advance whether there are any rules before you buy.)

- **Tubular-style device.** This is a very short metal tube that is slightly narrower at one end than the other. It is very similar in function to the sticht-plate device, although its rope-feeding action is smoother than that of its flattened cousin. The one major difference is that you must be certain to move your brake hand to the side to hold a fall (that is, you must make certain that the rope is not running parallel out of the device), because the device will not lock up otherwise. Advantage: it is lightweight and inexpensive, which makes it the most common type you'll see. Disadvantage: it really depends on the brake hand to stop the fall. Price range: $15 to $20.

- **Petzl Grigri:** This is a patented device that, once threaded, allows the free running of the rope as the climber ascends but locks up when there is a shock load (such as a falling climber). It works something like the seatbelt in your car—with smooth, slow movements, it moves freely; when tugged on hard, it locks

The three most common **belay devices**: tubular style (**A**), Grigri (**B**), and figure 8 (**C**).

up. The *Grigri* is the most popular device among sport climbers because it makes the duty of holding the rope while the climber hangs on the rope working out the moves a lot easier. Advantage: in the case of accidental loss of control of the brake hand on the rope, this device will still arrest the fall. Disadvantage: it's expensive. Price: about $70.

**Figure 8.** As the name implies, this device is shaped like the numeral 8 with the top part of the 8 being smaller than the bottom part. Although it is primarily used for rappelling, it can also be used for belaying. The rope can be threaded through the device in a couple of ways to create more or less friction; however, it is normally recommended to use the small end of the 8 like a sticht-plate device for belaying. Advantage: it's inexpensive and is the smoothest and most preferred device for rappelling. Disadvantage: like the sticht plate and tuber, it can only work if the belayer's hand remains on the rope in the case of a fall. Price range: $14 to $20.

**Sticht-type device.** Also referred to as a *sticht-plate*, this is a metal plate with two oval slots or openings that are just the right size to accept a *bight* (bend) of rope fed through it. Once the bight is fed through, it's clipped to a locking carabiner attached to your harness. In the event of a fall, the device locks the rope against the carabiner. Some are fitted with a spring on one side to prevent the device from locking up when it isn't needed. Advantage: this device is very lightweight and inexpensive, making it quite popular. Disadvantage: it takes some practice to become smooth in feeding out rope, and the belayer's brake hand on the rope is critical to holding the fall. Price range: $15 to $20.

These are the four most common devices, and you'll find that everyone has a personal preference and an opinion about which is best. Personally, I won't use anything but a Grigri. I always recommend it in situations where a smaller person (a woman, teenager, or child) is belaying and holding falls of people who are much heavier (most grown men). A falling climber who is quite a bit heavier than the belayer creates relatively higher forces (the *shock load*) on the belayer. At the extreme, this shock load could cause the belayer to lose control of her brake hand on the rope. The Grigri offers more security to a lighter belayer in this situation.

When you purchase your belay device, be sure to read the technical information that comes with it. Don't rely only on the written instructions or diagrams, however; be sure you're shown how to rig it correctly, as well as the proper belay technique for your device, by someone who knows what she's doing and is familiar with the device you've bought.

Caring for your belay device is quite simple: don't drop it. Aluminum can develop stress fractures if it is dropped any great distance onto rocks or anything hard. These stress fractures are not visible to the human eye, so your care will be in the prevention. Also, after years of lowering and rappelling with your device, it will probably develop wear grooves in the metal. Initially, grooves like this pose no real danger. Just be aware when they get to the stage of creating sharp edges, and use common sense: if the grooves get too pronounced, you'll want to retire it.

## GLOVES

Although they aren't a necessity for belaying, I highly recommend the use of gloves. Even though I never thought of using them in my earlier years of climbing—it wasn't cool or macho to protect your hands—I began using gloves for belaying after seeing that nearly everyone in Europe belays with gloves. Now I

## WHY TWO SLOTS?

• • • • • • • • • • • • • • •

The tubular device and the sticht-plate device have two slots in them; however, during most of your belaying, you'll only use one slot. You push a bight of rope through the slot, and you clip and lock your carabiner through that loop of rope that is now underneath the device. One end will go to the climber, and the other will be the end for your brake hand. The two slots are used at the same time either when you are rappelling or if you learn to belay when your climber is using two ropes when leading (known as *double rope technique*). Double rope technique is quite rare in North America. It typically is used only on alpine routes and in some traditional climbing.

find them absolutely essential to my belaying. Gloves are especially critical when using a Grigri because so much of the control of lowering the climber is dependent on the brake hand. Because I'm lighter than nearly everyone I climb with, the added security of a glove on my brake hand is reassuring. Not to mention, the abuse to your hands is eliminated with gloves. Most gloves have a loop sewn on each wrist so you can clip them to your harness when you're not using them.

Wearing gloves also reduces the risk of burning your hands (and possibly dropping your climber) in the event of a very severe fall. In extreme falls, when using nearly all of the belay devices mentioned in this chapter, the rope will begin to slip and start burning the belayer's hand at around 2 to 2.5 kilo Newtons (that's about 450 to 560 pounds of force). (The exception is the Grigri, which doesn't slip until 2,000 pounds of force.) Using gloves in a case such as this would protect both your hands and the climber you're belaying. There are special belay/rappel gloves that have triple-leather reinforced palms, so they're extra durable where they need to be. Prices range from $25 to $30.

## LOCKING CARABINER

The *locking carabiner* attaches the belay device to your harness. There are many different styles to choose from, and the main differences have to do with the size and shape of the frame and the locking mechanism. The most common shape for use with a belay device is the pear-shaped carabiner. I suggest buying a carabiner that fits your hand size—avoid super huge or super tiny carabiners.

The carabiner's locking mechanism is what prevents the gate from accidentally opening when you're belaying. There are a multitude of locking mechanisms, and I recommend checking out as many as you can. Let your tactile senses help select the right one. Hold the carabiner in your hand. Does it feel solid but light? Push the gate open with your thumb and let it snap back to the closed position. Is the gate action smooth and even in its operation? Play with the locking sleeve. Is it simple to use? Can you tell at a glance whether it's locked or unlocked? Carabiners can last for years and years (if you buy a good one), so make sure you get one that *feels* like quality. Prices range from $12 to $18.

## HELMET

Once again, comfort is key. If your helmet isn't comfortable, you're not going to want to wear the thing all day. You also want a helmet that has a sizing adjustment that is quick and easy to use. There are essentially two styles of helmets: the traditional, head-harness suspension and the newer, low-profile, bike helmet style. The traditional helmets are heavier but also more durable. You don't have to worry about dings or scratches, dropping the helmet, or other abuses. The newer low-profile helmets are much lighter and fit closer to the head.

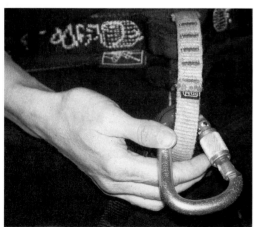

A locking carabiner correctly attached to the strongest part of the harness—the belay loop.

Two helmet styles: traditional (left) and low-profile (right).

However, they are more susceptible to cosmetic or even structural damage if not taken care of properly. They are similar to bike helmets in their construction, but they're designed to endure the Union Internationale des Associations d'Alpinisme (UIAA) tests for climbing helmets. (Please note: you may be tempted to use a helmet you already own for other sports—don't! Other helmets, even those that look like climbing helmets, have not been tested for the kinds of impact you may encounter in climbing.)

## Caring for your helmet

If you need to clean your helmet, use plain water. If it's really dirty, add a little mild liquid detergent to the water. Avoid corrosive substances or solvents, and do not store it in extreme temperatures.

You'll need to be aware of when to retire your helmet. The most obvious reason to stop using a helmet is if it is damaged due to rock fall or if you've landed on your head and cracked the shell. Even if there are no outward signs of damage to the shell but the impact was severe, you should replace it. After five years of use, a helmet should be replaced *even if it has never sustained a blow*. The materials themselves will weaken after this amount to time, although you may not be able to detect this weakness with visual inspection.

## ROPES

Once you start going outside on your own, you'll probably want to start buying enough gear to set up your own top ropes and eventually start leading. It's hard to stress the importance of your rope; the rope is what saves your life when you fall. Rope is the most important piece of gear to research and understand before you make a purchase. Rope also is one of the most expensive pieces of equipment, ranging from $130 to $180. You should know a little about how climbing ropes differ from other types of rope, how to interpret the test results on the hangtag, and which type, length, and diameter are right for you.

Modern climbing ropes are *kernmantle* ropes, a term which simply refers to the general construction of the rope. A climbing rope consists of a core (the *kern*), which is the primary load bearing part of the rope, surrounded by a protective sheath (the *mantle*). The main characteristic of climbing ropes that distinguishes them from all others is that they are *dynamic*—that is, they have dynamic or energy-absorbing qualities when shock loaded, which is what happens when a falling

• • • • • • • • • • • • • • • • • • • • • • • • • • •

**R**ope is the most important piece of gear to research and understand before you make a purchase.

• • • • • • • • • • • • • • • • • • • • • • • • • • •

climber comes to the end of the rope. The rope's ability to stop a climber's fall gently, to take some of the force out of the impact on the climber's protection, and to ease the impact on the belayer is achieved by the dynamic quality of the climbing rope. You want to make sure you buy a dynamic rope, not a static rope; both use *kernmantle* construction but static ropes are not safe for climbing falls because they have virtually no dynamic properties.

Climbing ropes are tested by the UIAA for a number of different criteria: impact force, number of falls withstood, weight, and static elongation. The tests that they subject climbing ropes to are far more severe than those climbers actually put their ropes through in real-life climbing situations. The most relevant test results will be printed on the hangtag of the ropes (actually a small manufacturer's brochure that includes a table with UIAA ratings), which provides you a fairly easy way to comparison shop. But what do the numbers mean?

The most important factor is a number called *impact force*. This number tells how much force is transmitted to the climber's body when she comes to the end of her fall. A tremendous amount of energy is created as a climber is falling. At the moment that the fall is stopped, the rope will absorb some of the force of that energy (the *shock load*). The rope's ability to absorb this energy is related to how it stretches over the course of the fall. A rope that does a good job will transmit lower impact force to the climber, her pro, and her belayer. For this reason, you'll want to look for a rope with low impact force numbers. These numbers are usually stated in kilo Newtons (kN). The maximum impact that the UIAA allows in a single rope is 12 kN, so you'll want a rope that is well under that number.

The next criteria to look at is the *number of falls held*. This is a test that is done by dropping an 80-kilogram weight over a carabiner edge in a fall that is meant to replicate a factor 2 fall (see the sidebar for a description of a factor 2 fall). This test is repeated until the rope breaks. It's probably quite obvious that you'll want to get a rope with a high number for this test. The UIAA's minimum requirement for number of falls held is five with a single rope.

The third factor to consider is the weight of the rope. This is usually stated in grams per meter. Once you've decided on a diameter (which I discuss below), you'll want to find a rope that is lightweight for its size. If you're comparing two ropes of equal diameter and the previous two test results are similar, choose the one that is lighter. Most likely the diameters will not be exact, but what's important to you as a climber is that you get the lightest rope that has the best impact force results and fall ratings.

There are two other numbers on the hangtag that are relatively less important: static elongation and sheath slippage. *Static elongation* is the amount the rope stretches under a static load; for normal climbing, this factor isn't too

core
(kern)

sheath
(mantle)

Kernmantle
climbing rope.

# FALL FACTORS

The severity of a climbing fall isn't related just to the length of the fall. More important in determining out how hard a fall is to the climber (and to her gear and belayer) is how long the fall was and how much rope was available to absorb the energy of the fall. We calculate this figure by dividing the length of the fall by the amount of rope from the belayer to the climber. Keep in mind that the job of a climbing rope is to take up the force that is generated when a climber falls. A small amount of rope means a small capacity to absorb the energy of the fall. This is best shown with the two examples shown here.

This calculation gives us the *fall factor*, which is the measurement of the severity of a fall. The worst-case-scenario fall in lead climbing is a factor 2 fall. This type of fall can only happen at a hanging belay when the climber has reached a point directly above the belay and then falls onto it without any intermediate protection point. This is an extraordinarily rare occurrence, but it is this factor 2 fall that is replicated in the rope testing labs to determine the *fall ratings*.

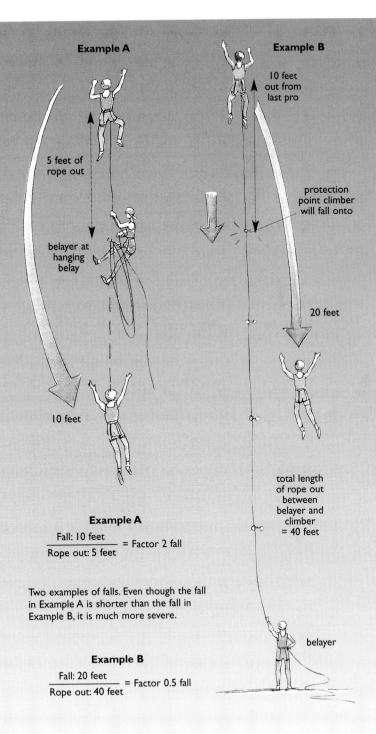

**Example A**

5 feet of rope out

belayer at hanging belay

10 feet

**Example A**

$$\frac{\text{Fall: 10 feet}}{\text{Rope out: 5 feet}} = \text{Factor 2 fall}$$

Two examples of falls. Even though the fall in Example A is shorter than the fall in Example B, it is much more severe.

**Example B**

$$\frac{\text{Fall: 20 feet}}{\text{Rope out: 40 feet}} = \text{Factor 0.5 fall}$$

**Example B**

10 feet out from last pro

protection point climber will fall onto

20 feet

total length of rope out between belayer and climber = 40 feet

belayer

critical, as long as it is under the UIAA maximum of 8 percent. *Sheath slippage*, the amount the sheath slips along the core, must be under 2 percent, but these days it's easy to find ropes with 0-percent sheath slippage.

The most common rope lengths are 50 meters and 60 meters. Deciding what length to get will be determined by where you intend to use the rope. If the climbing areas you frequent are shorter in height and you don't plan on traveling around to many different climbing areas, then a 50-meter rope is fine. If the standard-length rope for your nearest crags is 60 meters or you plan to travel around to different climbing areas, then you definitely should spend the extra money for a 60-meter rope. If you don't know, ask local climbers what they recommend.

Besides length, diameter is the other choice about size you'll make. Climbing ropes come in diameters ranging from around 8 to 11 millimeters. The skinnier diameters, however, are *double* or *half* ropes, which are used in pairs for ice and alpine routes or for extreme rock routes with marginal pro or placements that zigzag. Most rock climbers use *single* ropes, a characteristic that is designated by the numeral 1 in a circle on the tape at the rope's ends. The choice of diameter for single ropes ranges from around 9.4 to 11 millimeters. Choosing a diameter depends on the type of climbing you plan to do. For those who mainly sport climb—where the climber falls fairly frequently, the falls are clean, and the rope is rarely dragged over the rock—a smaller diameter rope (9.4 to 10 millimeters) is preferred. Thinner ropes weigh less; they also handle nicely for belaying and have lower impact forces, so the falls are softer. For primarily trad climbing and top roping—where the rope may be subjected to more abrasion over rock but the climber is falling less often—most people choose a 10.5- or 11-millimeter rope. The most popular diameter by far is 10.5 millimeters because most climbers are seeking a good compromise.

One option available on ropes is a *dry treatment*, which is a coating or substance that is impregnated into the nylon of the rope to help prevent absorption of water. Nearly all ice climbers and mountaineers use dry ropes because they travel over snow and ice. There is some climbing mythology about dry ropes having greater abrasion resistance, but there has been no conclusive proof of this. In my two years of working for a rope manufacturer, I seriously came to doubt this belief. For rock climbing, dry treatment is an added expense you don't really need.

## Caring for your rope

Climbing ropes are exceptionally strong and have been tested to simulate the most extreme circumstances a climber encounters. In fact, there has never been an incident of a modern kernmantle rope spontaneously breaking in an actual climbing fall. However, climbing ropes are terribly fragile if not used properly. Even a rope with exceptional UIAA test results will cut like butter if it is run over a sharp edge and weighted. The unfortunate truth is that a weighted rope is very susceptible to cutting. Nearly all accidents that involved a rope breaking were because of either a fall where the rope contacted a sharp flake on impact or a fall where the rope was running over an unprotected edge while the climbers were rappelling or top roping. For this reason, it is paramount that you always be mindful of where the rope is running—especially for top ropes, rappels, and anytime there are sharp flakes or angles that you might be falling on.

Other basic precautions include the following.

1.　　Limit extended exposure to the sun because UV rays hasten the deterioration of nylon. Store your rope in a cool, dry place.

2.　　Avoid contact with corrosives (such as battery acid) or any solvents (such as fingernail polish remover). I recommend keeping your rope away from *any* other chemicals because you don't know what the effect might be.

3.　　Don't step on your rope (or anyone else's) because this can grind dirt and debris into the core.

4.　　Periodically check your rope over thoroughly. A visual and manual inspection of the entire length of the rope should be made to look for tears or serious abrasion spots and to feel for any deformation of the core, such as flat spots and nodules. If you find any irregularities like this, the rope should be retired.

5.　　You should also retire your rope when you can see any of the white core showing through the sheath, if 50 percent or more of the sheath strands are broken, if you take a single, very severe fall on it, or if it's more than five years old.

6.　　If your rope gets really dirty, you can wash it. If you want to use a machine, go to the laundromat and use one of those front-loading, nonagitating washers. I usually wash mine in the bathtub. Use clear, very lukewarm or even cold water. If the rope is super grimy, add a little bit of mild soap. Do not use bleach. Once the rope has been thoroughly rinsed, hang it loosely from some furniture or lay it out on your bedroom floor or outside on the grass under the shade of a tree. Don't ever put it in the dryer; air-drying is the only acceptable method.

7.　　When you first uncoil a new rope, be sure to do it correctly so you avoid kinks. Once the rope is out of its packaging, don't flake it out like you normally do for laying a rope out. Instead, reverse the procedure the manufacturer used to coil it in the first place. Hold the rope with both your arms through the center of the loops of the coil; then begin unwinding the rope as you might a garden hose.

## Using a rope bag

One of the more recent innovations in climbing gear is a rope bag, which will cost somewhere between $35 and $45. Goodness only knows why it took modern climbers over three decades to figure out such a wonderful yet very simple way to care for and carry climbing ropes. A rope bag is used to store and carry your rope and to keep it out of the dirt when you lay it at the base of a climb. The rope bag virtually eliminates the need to coil and uncoil your rope each time you go climbing. Instead, the rope remains flaked out inside this bag. When you get to the base of the climb, you open the bag and unroll the built-in tarp, locate the top of the rope (which you've tied

Rope bag.

to a colored tab on the inside of the tarp so you can find it easily), and voilá, you're ready to climb.

When you're finished climbing, the rope gets flaked back into the tarp, which you then fold into the attached bag part of the rope bag and then pull the drawstring cord and compression straps to tighten it compactly. You then sling the padded carrying strap over your shoulder and away you go. The greatest advantage of a rope bag is keeping your rope clean in areas where the ground at the base of the cliff is very dusty or muddy.

## Coiling a rope

Even if you use a rope bag, there will be times when you'll need to coil your rope. A properly coiled rope is a pleasure to use, whereas a sloppy job of coiling can be a complete nightmare to deal with. Learning to coil a rope is a fairly simple thing, but it's a skill that takes a little practice so you don't end up doing a poor job of it. There are several different methods for coiling a rope; however, the single-strand butterfly coil shown opposite in example 1 is the most popular way to coil and is, in my humble opinion, the best. This coil is superior because it doesn't need to be flaked out to be ready to use. You simply undo the finishing knots that secure the coils and lay it out.

## A TYPICAL RACK OF GEAR

At some point, you may want to start acquiring a lead climbing rack. You'll also need some of the following gear for setting up top ropes outside.

- **Slings**
  4 to 6 2-foot slings, $6 each
  10-foot to 30-foot 1-inch webbing for anchors
  (for slinging trees and boulders), $3 to $10 each

- **Carabiners and draws**
  4 locking biners, $10 to $18 each
  6 to 8 regular gate biners, $5 to $12 each
  10 to 14 quickdraws (2 biners with a sewn webbing sling in between),
  $15 to $25 each

- **Passive protection**
  wired stoppers, $6 to $8 each
  hexentrics, $15 to $25 each

(continued page 138)

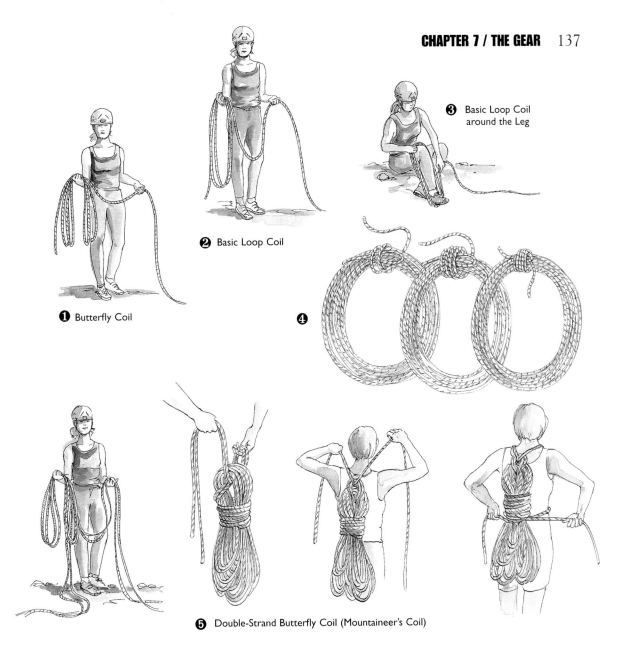

**2** Basic Loop Coil

**3** Basic Loop Coil around the Leg

**1** Butterfly Coil

**4**

**5** Double-Strand Butterfly Coil (Mountaineer's Coil)

Three single-strand methods to coil a rope. **1.** The **Butterfly Coil** is the best method for coiling a rope because the rope feeds freely. Begin the coil at one end, pulling one arm length from the pile, and bend the strand to form a loop, then drape it over one side of your hand. Drape the next loop over the other side of your hand. Continue alternating the loops until you have about 5 feet of rope left. With this remaining rope you'll tie a finishing knot (4). **2. Basic Loop.** Beginning at one end of the rope, pull one arm length from the pile and form a loop with the strand by laying it over your other hand. Continue stacking these circular loops into your hand until you have about 5 feet of rope left. Finish the coil (4). **3. Basic Loop Coil around the Leg.** This is essentially the same as #2, except you form the loops by wrapping the strand of rope around your knee and foot. This method is popular because it makes loops uniform in length and is less taxing on the arms. **4. Finishing the coil.** With the 5-foot tail, form a bight of rope and lay it atop the coils (where you're holding the rope). Begin wrapping the rest of the tail around the coils over the place where the bight is. When you have 4–6 wraps, feed the tail through the bight and tighten the bight by pulling on the strand that's now on the other side of the wraps. **5. Double-Strand Butterfly Coil** (also called the **Mountaineer's Coil**). Find and grasp both ends of the rope together in one hand. From the pile, pull an arm's length of rope, which will be a double strand, and bend it to form a loop. Drape this loop across one side of your hand. Drape the next double-stranded loop you pull up on the other side. Continue alternating loops until 12–15 feet of rope are left. To finish the coil, wrap the remaining tail around the middle of the drapes of loops, working toward the top of the coils. When you have 4–6 wraps, pass a bight of rope through the hole at the top. Thread the remainder of the tail through this bight. Use the two strands to lash the coil job onto your shoulders and around your waist, like a pack.

## WHO YA GONNA TRUST?

Many of the employees of climbing shops are themselves climbers, some very experienced. However, if you ask them a technical "use" question, they will tell you, in some diplomatic way, that they can't tell you—even if they know the proper and correct use of the product. Telling a customer how to adjust a backpack to fit or showing her how to put up a tent she's about to buy is acceptable. After all, you can't kill or maim yourself if your pack fits poorly or your tent poles are in the wrong sleeves. With climbing gear, however, especially in the United States, stores must protect themselves from the possible liability of telling a customer how to use a product. This is why you will always be directed to the manufacturer's *technical use and care notice*, which should come with the product. If you're considering buying a product and you're not sure of its use or care, ask to see this notice if the salesperson doesn't offer it. If the store doesn't have one, find out whether there is some *official manufacturer's* document like this for that product. If there isn't, you probably should choose another brand.

As strange as it may sound, there isn't really a specific watchdog organization for the climbing industry that makes certain that the climbing consumer is protected. It is up to the individual manufacturers to decide whether they want to get their products UIAA or CE (Comité Européan, the standards committee of the European Union) approved, whether they want to stamp their minimum breaking strengths on their products, or whether they actually state their UIAA or CE test results truthfully. It's up to you, as the customer, to make certain you're buying a reliable and well-tested product. I encourage you to follow these guidelines:

1.   Only buy gear that has been UIAA or CE approved. The UIAA and the CE are the international organizations that set the testing criteria and (through independent labs) test and approve climbing equipment. If you don't see the UIAA or CE mark on the product, ask the salesperson or look on the hangtag.

2.   Always buy name-brand gear, even if it's a bit more expensive. It shouldn't be too hard to figure out which ones are the top brands—just look at the climbing magazines or ask the salespeople. The top brands belong to the companies who have been around for a long time (and who *will* be around for a long time). Not only have their products withstood the test of real-life climbing, but these companies have also spent the time and money necessary to stringently test their new products in their own labs as well as pay the fees to have them tested and approved by the UIAA or CE. These companies will also be there to back up their products in case of warrantied defects.

3.   The old adage "you get what you pay for" is just as true with climbing equipment as it is with anything else—possibly more so. Climbing gear is life-safety equipment. It is what protects you from death or injury when you fall. Unless your life isn't worth very much, don't buy the cheapest gear possible. When you buy quality equipment, it will last and it will work when you need it.

*(continued from page 136)*

●   **Camming devices**
     quad cams, $60 to $70 each
     tri cams, $50 to $60 each

●   **Other pieces**
     gear sling, $20 each
     nut tool, $8 to $12 each

# Chapter 8

## GETTING FIT, STAYING SAFE, AND HAVING FUN

To really enjoy the sport of climbing, it's important that you feel fit and avoid injury. In the first part of this chapter, I describe how you can get stronger, prevent injuries, and be smart about recovery if you do get injured. In the second part, I show how good judgment, preparation, and knowledge can help you avoid unnecessary risks and accidents. One goal in climbing, aside from having a ton of fun, is to stay alive and healthy.

### GETTING STRONGER

I'm often asked, "How can I get stronger for climbing?" I'm a firm believer that the best way to increase your strength for climbing is by climbing. There are very few exercises or weight-training regimens that translate well to climbing. However, if you do feel that you could use a little boost to your upper body strength, I suggest you focus on body-weight exercises, such as pull-ups and bar dips. There are climbing-specific *fingerboards* or *hang boards* made by some of the climbing hold manufacturers, such as Metolius and Pusher. These boards offer a variety of holds from which to hang that are meant to simulate climbing holds. These boards are ideal for working on your pull-ups and doing finger-strengthening hanging and pulling exercises. My first recommendation for training, however, is to concentrate on climbing. Your best bet for getting fit is to incorporate some training games into your indoor climbing sessions.

● ● ● ● ● ● ● ● ● ● ● ● ● ● ● ● ● ● ● ● ● ● ● ● ●

**Y**our best bet for getting fit is to
incorporate some training games
into your indoor climbing sessions.

● ● ● ● ● ● ● ● ● ● ● ● ● ● ● ● ● ● ● ● ● ● ● ● ●

According to Bobbi Bensman, 38, a former National Champion with more 5.13 routes to her credit than any other American female: "Some people might think I'm crazy, but I love getting pumped . . . you know that deep-down, aching, burning feeling you get in your forearms. Of course, I like it when it happens when I'm training, but I hate it if it happens on a climb! I suppose you could say it's a love-hate thing."

## Training games for the gym

## Climbing 'til you drop

Find a wall that has several routes of varying degrees of difficulty that can all be top roped with one rope. Start by climbing a route that is quite hard for you, something right at your limit. Don't worry if you fall off. The moment you get lowered to the ground, start up the next easiest route. Then continue until you're completely pumped. You should strive to do four to five climbs in a row. Once you've finished with this cycle, give yourself a short, designated rest period of between five and ten minutes (depending on your existing fitness level). Then repeat the set. In the beginning, start out with two or three sets. Once you've increased your endurance, you can do four or even five of these cycles.

## Adding on and variations

*Add-on* is a training game that requires two or more partners; the preferred number of participants is three or four. In the bouldering area of the gym, one person will start the game by making up a sequence of a certain number of moves—usually three to five moves depending on the size of the group. The more people you have, the fewer moves each individual will make up. Each climber, in succession, "adds on" moves to the sequence created by the climber before her. For example, let's say there are three people and each person must add on four moves. The first climber begins by making a sequence of four moves. The second climber then does the first person's four-move sequence and adds four more to that for a total of eight moves. The third person then does those eight moves and adds her own four-move sequence for a total of twelve moves. Then the sequence rotates back to the first person, who must now do the twelve moves and create four more moves, and so on.

The great thing about this exercise is that you'll end up doing different styles of moves than you would normally make up for yourself. A slight variation of this game would be to limit the length of the overall problem. After the bouldering route gets to be a certain length, say twenty-four moves, you'll drop the starting four moves off the front each time four moves is added to the end.

## Pointing

On the bouldering wall, your partner will indicate to you a starting hold to begin the "climb." From there, she'll point to the next handhold you must go to and tell you which hand you must use on it. The climber can use whatever footholds she wants. The climber should refrain from matching on the holds (see page 90), except when the pointer says she can. The pointer should be careful to not make moves that are too extreme because she doesn't want the climber to fall off too early in the game. If the pointer does make moves that are near the climber's limit, she should follow those with a few moves that the climber can recover on. The goal is to stay on the wall as long as possible for a great endurance workout.

## Targeting weaknesses

This exercise also requires a partner. You and your partner will confess your climbing weaknesses to each other. A weakness can be a certain type of hold you feel weak on, such as pinches or pockets. Or, it can be a certain angle, such as overhangs or slabs. It also can be certain types of moves, such as drop knees or cross-through moves. In the bouldering area, you and your partner will make boulder problems for each other that target the other's weaknesses. This is a great way to face the very things you need to work on most.

## Making up boulder problems

Again, the bouldering area is a great location for this exercise. Create boulder problems that feature mostly one type of hold. This is another really good way to strengthen your weaknesses. For example, create a problem that uses mostly pockets. Or, if you're weak on slopers or pinches, make the problem using mostly those types of holds. The problems can be short with harder moves (from 4 to 8 moves) or longer route-style problems (from 8 to 20 moves). Don't worry if you can't find a hold that fits with the style for every move, as long as the majority of the holds do.

### Training with fingerboard exercises

Besides climbing itself, training on a fingerboard is probably the best way to increase your strength for climbing. Be sure to warm up slowly and well before doing any of the exercises suggested below. To warm up, do several sets of just hanging your body weight from the biggest holds, follow with assisted pull-ups, and then ultimately do a couple of pull-ups on the biggest holds. Once you've warmed up, you'll still want to begin by doing the easy exercises first; save the hardest of the exercises until you feel well warmed up.

Exercises to perform on a fingerboard include the following.

1.    **Simple pull-ups on the biggest holds.** Do four or five sets with as many pull-ups as you can do in each set.

2.    **Pull-ups on smaller holds and pockets.** You may need to take some weight off by having a friend hold your feet or your waist or by making use of a chair to push off with your feet.

3.    **Timed hanging-on holds.** Hang from different holds for a set period of time. Start out by hanging for 20 seconds and when you've mastered that, increase the

Fingerboard.

hanging time to as much as two minutes per hold. Start out on the biggest holds and do three sets of hangs at your designated time. Go down to the next smallest holds and do the same thing. You can vary this by doing as many sets as needed to get to the point of not being able to hang on for the entire designated time. You can also make this harder by limiting the amount of rest between sets; for example, try resting only one minute between sets.

4.    **Hanging to pull-ups.** In this exercise, you'll hang on medium-sized holds for a designated amount of time (say 20 seconds); then from the hanging position, you'll do as many pull-ups as you can. Once you let go, time your rest; 45 seconds to 1 minute 30 seconds is a good starting range. Then repeat the whole exercise. When you can't hold the hanging position for the designated time, switch to the next largest holds and repeat the exercise.

5.    **Changing to different holds while on the board.** While hanging on one set of holds, you'll move one hand at a time to a different hold. This isn't as easy as it sounds. To do this, you need to pull up a little on the holds to unweight them so you can let go for a moment with one hand. Start out on the bigger holds and then move to the smaller ones.

6.    **Other exercises limited only by your imagination.** If you can get together with a friend, it will make your workout more fun. Remember in the beginning to do all the exercises on the big holds; this way you'll avoid injury and be able to do the exercises. As you get stronger, you'll be able to work your way down to smaller holds. Also, if you can't do these exercises by yourself initially, have a partner take weight off by holding you at your waist or your feet. This same effect can be achieved alone by tying some surgical tubing with a loop at the bottom (or use the commercial version of this called the *Sport Cord*) to the board itself. Using this prop, you can put your foot in the loop and push yourself up to take some of the weight off.

## PREVENTING AND HANDLING INJURIES

Warming up is the best way to prevent injuries. As I described in chapter 6, warming up will also help you climb better, so you should always include it. Spending 15 to 20 minutes stretching is an ideal way to get some blood flowing and to increase your flexibility. In your stretching, be sure to do some upper body, forearms, and finger stretches, because these are the muscle groups you'll be using most.

Very few people know how to warm up properly. Too often I see people warming up on routes that are very close to their limit. They struggle, get pumped, and risk injuring themselves. This is not warming up. The ideal climbing warm-up would include some light, gentle stretching, fol-

> **W**arming up is the best way to prevent injuries.

lowed by hanging from some big holds at the base of the climb, bouldering on easy terrain, or climbing on a very, very easy route. If there isn't a route that is easy enough, do just the beginning of it and lower off when it starts to become too hard. Bouldering around on big holds is also a good way to start getting the blood flowing. I recommend doing at least two, preferably three, routes that are well below your maximum level. I often do at least four warm-up routes before trying my hardest climb of the day. Here's an example of the routes you'd climb if you were warming up to climb a 5.11a, which was the hardest you'd ever climbed: you would start by doing a 5.9, an easy 5.10, and then a 5.10b or c.

Injuries can also be avoided by knowing when to call it quits. At the end of the day, if you're feeling really tired and exhausted but think you'll benefit by doing "just one more route," you may be better off to just skip it. If you do decide to do one more, make it super easy—a cooldown route. Very tired muscles make for an ideal situation for tendons to get pulled or torn, in addition to breeding *tendonitis* (an overuse injury).

Also, be aware of holds that make your fingers or forearms feel tweaked or that put too much pressure or unnatural stress on your shoulder or wrist joints. One-finger pockets, shallow two-finger pockets, very thin edges, and any hold that isolates your fingers all require you to be very well warmed up and should always be taken with some caution. When you encounter these types of holds, be very aware of your body's signals—if something feels "funny," let go. Don't worry about falling; the result of a tendon pull is far more devastating than not doing the route.

If you feel as if your fingers or wrists are weak and prone to injury or if you have injured them before and are just getting back into climbing, you may want to tape preventatively. The finger joints can be taped in between the joints; for this you will want to use one continuous narrow strip (¼ to ½ inch) of cloth athletic tape per finger. Don't hinder the flexion of the joint or the circulation of blood to the finger, but do wrap the tape tautly enough that the joint is supported. Wrists can be taped with a simple horizontal wrapping, again taking care not to cut off flexion or circulation but still making sure the wrapping is firmly supportive. You'll have to use some judgment here, and experience will teach you what tension is right.

For crack climbing, you will probably want to tape to protect the backs of your hands. There is only one type of tape to use for this: cloth athletic tape. You'll want to buy it in the 1½-inch width. There are several different taping methods, one that virtually covers the entire hand, including the knuckles and wrists. I've never favored this *tape glove*, as it is known; instead, I prefer a simple wrapping of the most used parts of the hand.

For all taping, be sure that you flex your hand while applying the tape so that you don't get the wrap too tight. If you want extra protection, you can put strips of tape on the backs of the

Left: Taping fingers to prevent injury: tape knuckles and wrists separately. **Above:** Taping hands for crack climbing. **Below left:** Steps for a thorough tape job.

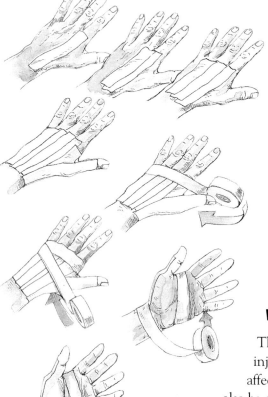

hands before beginning the wrapping. For a simple tape job for crack climbing, start inside your hand, near the crotch of your thumb. Wrap the tape over the crotch of your thumb and angle it back toward your outside wrist bone. Then wrap it around the underside of your wrist, heading toward the base of the thumb. Once you've taped around the base of the thumb, wrap the tape diagonally right across the top of your hand and go around the outside edge of the palm between the wrist and the big joint of the pinkie finger. Now you'll be back on the palm and can do a couple more wraps in the same fashion. Finish up with a couple of wraps on the wrist area, making sure that you bend your wrist as you wrap it.

## What to do if you get injured

The most common injuries by far will be overuse injuries such as tendonitis. The fingers are particularly affected, but sometimes elbows and even shoulders can also be affected. You may also experience a more traumatic type of injury, such as a muscle, tendon, or ligament tear; fortunately, these injuries are less common in climbing. If your trauma is severe, you may end up away from climbing for a while and in physical therapy. However, if you do suffer an injury such as tendonitis or minor muscle or tendon tears, I have some advice for taking charge of your own recovery. Most of this advice is anecdotal, and I must state that I am neither a doctor nor a physical therapist. I have, however, suffered plenty of injuries as well as the consequences of not being smart about how to handle them. After years, I finally figured out how to deal with my injuries. I have also traded injury solutions with countless climbers as we all sought to get back to climbing and avoid further damage. Here are some of my ground rules for coming back from injury.

- **Stop climbing.** It's obvious that you need to stop climbing until any swelling or inflammation goes away or if you're experiencing acute pain even when not using the affected area. You can help reduce inflammation by icing the area and by using over-the-counter anti-inflammatories, such as Motrin and Advil. Once any immediate pain has dissipated, you should still avoid using the area for another week to 10 days or so.

- **Start with some physical therapy.** For finger injuries, use Chinese balls (for developing hand dexterity), squeeze tennis balls, or get some of that putty used for physical therapy. I've also used thick rubber bands and done resistance exercises with my hands and fingers. For elbows and shoulders, do resistance exercises with a Sport Cord or a loop of surgical tubing attached to a door. Do this for about a week before resuming climbing, and continue doing it for another two to three weeks after you've resumed climbing.

- **Begin climbing very easy routes with big holds.** Resist the temptation to climb anything that is even close to your level when you sustained the injury. Spend at least two weeks climbing at this reduced level. The third week you can increase the level, but still stick to routes with fairly big holds. In the fourth week, if your body is still feeling OK, you can bump the level up. Regardless of the grade of the route, if you encounter *any* hold that seems to be stressing the injured area, let go! Do not use it! You can actually climb a lot this way, but you must use restraint and good judgment.

On this program you can be back to nearly full speed in about two months. You may still need to favor the injured area by avoiding holds that hurt it for at least six months and by taping for prevention of further injury. If you retweak it during the recovery cycle, you'll have to take a few days off and start back at the beginning with physical therapy and easy climbing.

The surprising thing I have found is that prolonged rest (that is, no climbing at all for three to six months) is no better than resuming climbing sooner but at an easy level. In fact, my ultimate recovery has been faster on this program, and I've heard the same thing from many other climbers who have suffered these kinds of injuries.

• • • • • • • • • • • • • • • • • • • • • • • • • •

"**B**e able and willing to back off
a route that is too hard or just
doesn't feel right that day."

—Bobbi Bensman, veteran climber

• • • • • • • • • • • • • • • • • • • • • • • • • •

Bobbi Bensman's attitude is a good one, I think: "Choosing routes that are within your abilities, having the right equipment, knowing the climb and descent, and being realistic about the risks are all important factors. Knowledge is definitely power. Finally, be able and willing to back off a route that is too hard or just doesn't feel right that day. I can always boost my confidence after a fearful day of climbing by going back to old favorites or routes that are easy for me and just climbing for mileage and fun!"

## AVOIDING POTENTIAL HAZARDS

As you will hear quite often in this sport, accidents are mainly caused by human error rather than by objective hazards, such as rock fall and equipment failure. The best way to avoid accidents is to use good judgment. Finding climbing partners with solid skills, using common sense, and not being afraid to back off when you have a bad feeling about something are all part of staying alive and healthy.

With the popularity of climbing these days, I often see the proverbial "mistake waiting to happen" when I'm at popular crags or even in the gym. It's usually inexperience, ignorance, or both that lead to accidents. As a beginning climber, one of the smartest things you can do is to be aware of the people, places, and things that could lead to disaster. Here are some warning signs and situations to watch out for.

### People

- If you see people with an unusually large amount of gear and ropes at a top roping or bouldering area, with lots of brand new gear, or with trad climbing gear racked up at a sport climbing area, stay clear. These types of people are usually trying to look the part of a climber, but many times they have very little actual climbing experience. If they do have experience, it's usually gear centered and they have very little skill in moving on rock. They may talk a big game but struggle on relatively easy climbs.

- Be wary of climbing with people whose only "climbing" skills were learned in the military. The climbing techniques taught in the military are quite different from what the average rock climber uses. Unless they've had some further training in the civilian sector, they may not be good choices for climbing partners.

- Beware of people who tell you that they climb, but then you discover that what they do is a lot of rappelling. These types of people are probably not really climbers. They are *sport rappellers*, and at times when they cannot get to the top of the cliff on foot, they will climb to the top to set up their rappel lines. There's nothing wrong with sport rappelling per se, but it is one of the more dangerous things to do in climbing. Nearly all *real* climbers avoid rappelling whenever possible.

**The best way to avoid accidents is to use good judgment.**

- If you see people who are lazy belayers, you'd be smart not to climb with them. *Lazy belayers* are people who rarely look up to keep track of the climber's progress and who often leave a giant loop of slack in the rope while taking in or feeding out rope to the climber. The worst offense of lazy belayers is letting go of the brake hand to do other things, such as dig in their packs, eat, put a jacket on, and so on. People like this rarely become diligent belayers until they have an accident. Don't take a chance.

- Do not climb with people who are using homemade gear. Some people think they're going to save some money by sewing their own harnesses, making their own wired stoppers, or sewing their own webbing slings. I once witnessed a climber who fell to the ground from about 25 feet up. He had hooked up with a climbing partner he had just met that morning. The partner gave this poor young man his quickdraws to lead the pitch but neglected to tell him that they were home-sewn draws. When the guy fell, the seams of the quickdraw all blew out and he ended up hitting the ground instead of coming to the end of the rope. He escaped with both ankles broken but fortunately still alive to learn a hard lesson. This practice is beyond foolish and is courting disaster. Familiarize yourself with what commercially manufactured gear looks like—especially sewn gear—so you can recognize homemade gear when you see it.

- Be cautious about climbing with strangers—especially in trad climbing situations. Sometimes it's difficult to find climbing partners to go outside. When you're just starting out, you need to go with partners who can lead or who at least have the necessary skills to set up top rope anchors. At this stage, however, you cannot judge another person's abilities in this regard. Often you can find climbing partners quite readily at some of the destination crags, such as Yosemite and Joshua Tree. However, without knowing the person through a friend or getting an introduction from someone who is an experienced climber, you're taking a chance with your own life. I've seen many people with shoddy, unsafe climbing practices climbing and belaying at crags all over the country. Even if these unknown people have climbed for many years, they may have just gotten lucky and never had to test their safety systems. Be cautious in your choice of climbing partners.

## Places

- In areas where people or animals might be above you, always wear a helmet. The chances are greater of rock fall or other objects being thrown or knocked from the top of the cliff in areas with a lot of tourists. Also, after rain and thundershowers be aware that rocks and other debris could be falling down even without people around.

- Be very aware of the quality and solidity of the rock you are pulling on. There are many great climbing areas that have some bad rock, and there are a quite a few accidents that happen when a climber pulls a chunk of rock off while climbing. In lucky cases, the climber falls off and nothing else happens. Other, less fortunate cases range from the climber clobbering herself in the face or chest with the rock that has come off to the belayer getting conked with the falling rock. Always test questionable holds for hollowness by tapping them with your fingers or the heel of your hand, and visually inspect for cracks where the hold is attached to the wall.

- Always be certain when you are belaying a leading climber that you stand as close to the wall as is feasible and directly under the line of the climber. For traditional climbs, you should be tied off to an anchor point as well. The force of a falling climber, when you stop the fall with the belay device, will nearly always cause you to be pulled upward a bit. If the climber is quite a bit heavier than you are, you will be pulled up a lot. If you're standing too far away from the line of the climber, you will be abruptly pulled into the wall, which typically ends when you smash into it. Not life-threatening, perhaps, but I have seen people get injured this way. (See illustration page 112.)

- Keep the rope out of range of potential falling rock while belaying. Usually it's best to have it close to the wall and to one side of your belay stance.

- Descents are frequently the stage for more accidents than the actual climbing, so pay careful attention while descending a climb. If you get to the top of the route and you're cold or hungry or nightfall is approaching, you should be extra, extra cautious. Haste and fatigue can lead to poor judgment. Be sure you know where the descent is so you're not caught trying to figure it out in the dark. Either read the guidebook or ask someone who's done the route before, and try to scope it out from the ground before you start climbing. If the descent involves steep slabs that are wet or covered in gravel or pea-sized rocks, take your time or find a safer route. Don't attempt to down climb without a belay anywhere that a slip could result in a serious tumble or a long drop to the ground.

    If the descent involves rappelling, you'll want to double-check all your systems: Is the rappel device rigged properly? (Have your partner check it for you, too.) Is your locking carabiner locked? (Reach down and press on the gate.) Does the anchor look sound (with fresh-looking

**Your** safety is only as sure as the gear you use.

webbing slings, solid bolts, and rap rings that aren't too worn through)? You'll also want to make sure, on long rappels or rappels of uncertain length, that you've tied the two ends of the rope together with a big overhand or figure 8 knot to prevent accidentally rappelling off the end of the rope. When you arrive at the next rappel station, be sure that, once you're secured to it and are ready to de-rig your rappel, you are stable and have a tight grasp on your rappel device so that you don't drop it as you de-rig.

## Things

### Badly worn gear

Your safety is only as sure as the gear you use. Here is a list of gear and the signs of wear and tear that indicate it should be retired:

- **Ropes.** Avoid using ropes that are super fuzzy, have irregularities (such as flat spots or nodules that can be felt in the core), have tears in the sheath, or have sections where you can see the white core strands through the sheath. Don't use a rope that has held a very serious high-impact fall, even if it appears to be in new condition. Don't buy a used rope; you don't know its history.

- **Webbing.** Nylon webbing—whether slings for setting up anchors, the belt and leg loops of your harness, or quickdraws for clipping bolts—will deteriorate rapidly with sun exposure and abrasion. Signs that webbing shouldn't be used include the following: if it's very stiff, if the color has faded, if it shows signs of friction in the form of melted-looking areas, or if it shows signs of abrasion, such as fuzziness or an irregular texture or pattern.

- **Carabiners.** Since carabiners are made from aircraft aluminum alloys, they are slower to wear out than the gear made of nylon. However, they too suffer from age and abuse and need to be retired when they show such signs. Look for tiny cracks around the carabiner's *nose* (the nonhinged side where the gate and the frame of the carabiner meet when the gate closes), gates that are stiff and hard to get open, gates that are too soft and no longer offer any resistance when opening, gates that stick open or stick closed, gates that sound gritty when opening, or deep grooves worn in the well part of the carabiner frame from repeated lowering. These are all reasons to clip into something else.

## Rope directly on webbing

Never, ever, ever run ropes directly through nylon webbing or accessory cord for lowering a person on that rope. This is a most dangerous situation because a rope that is lowering a person will literally melt right through the sling and break it. For top ropes and for lowering someone, the rope should be running only through carabiners or *screwlinks* (which are similar to carabiners, but they screw closed rather than having a gate that opens and closes).

## Found gear

You'll never know the history of a piece of gear you find lying on the ground, so avoid using it, especially if you suspect it was dropped from a great height. You may find a single carabiner on a bolt or some other gear halfway up a climb; it was probably left as a *bail biner* or a *bail anchor* (gear left behind when someone was unable to finish the route). This gear is probably fine to use, but inspect it thoroughly.

## Old slings at rappel stations

If you get to a rappel anchor and see that all of the nylon slings are faded and stiff, they have lost much of their strength. You should add one of yours to the anchor and descend from that. You're better off going to buy yourself a new one to replace it than being carried out on a stretcher.

## Fixed gear

Often you'll be required to use old fixed *pitons* (tapered steel wedge hammered into the rock) or other fixed gear—such as bolts or even wired stoppers—that has been left in a crack. This gear may be perfectly safe, but use it only after you have given it a visual inspection. If you are in doubt of the safety of the fixed gear, be sure to back it up if possible with some natural gear that you place yourself; this way, if the fixed gear in question were to fail, you would still be safe. Look for the following in each situation:

- Pitons should be firm in their placement; make sure they haven't taken too many falls and have bent or cracked as a result.

- All bolts should be inspected for signs of obvious aging; excessive rusting is a strong clue. When you're clipping a carabiner into a bolt hanger and the hanger spins, the nut holding the hanger on may just need to be tightened, which you can usually do with your fingers. Don't worry that the bolt has been only finger tightened because it is the sheer strength of the bolt that gives it its strength; the nut simply stops the hanger from coming off the end of the bolt.

- Wired stoppers that are in a crack may have been left there intentionally or simply couldn't be removed by the last climbing party who did the route. Before using one, make sure the wires of the cable aren't broken and that the piece will still hold a fall.

## Improper gear

Whatever you do, don't ever use a static rope or any other type of rope not specifically designed for climbing; always buy dynamic kernmantle ropes created specifically to absorb the impact force that is generated in climbing falls.

**Extricating yourself from a potentially dangerous situation can save your life or your partner's life.**

## A single piece of gear

If there ever comes a time when you and your partner simply *must* get off the piece of rock you're on—whether it be a huge thunderstorm or you are in a self-rescue situation—never trust your safety to just one piece of gear. Always use at least two pieces of protection before you commit your weight to the anchor you have just created. That rule goes for natural pro you place, bolts and pitons that have been left in the rock, and any combination of bolts and natural gear.

Roxanna Brock, who is a climbing guide, first ascensionist—that is, first person to establish a climb—and veteran of countless sport and trad climbs, including big walls, talks about fear: "Fear is normal; it's what alerts us to potential danger. I use my fear as an indicator: do I need to back off here, am I in over my head or do I just need to place another piece? Sometimes it really helps heighten my awareness, so my focus is where it needs to be. I never disregard my fear—it might be trying to tell me something important."

### GETTING YOURSELF OUT OF A BAD SITUATION

Even if you have followed all of the precautions outlined above, you may still find yourself in jeopardy through no mistake of your own. Extricating yourself from a potentially dangerous situation can save your life or your partner's life. Here are some ways to get back to safe ground.

### Down climbing

Sometimes you may end up in over your head, and being adept at down climbing may be your safest solution. Perhaps the guidebook wasn't clearly written and you're on a route that's beyond your climbing abilities. You may have strayed off the route without realizing it. Or maybe the crux move of the boulder problem you're on is right near the top and the landing at the base is sloping or piled with boulders. These are situations when you'll want to reverse the climbing you've already done. This reversal is not as simple as it sounds; trust me, climbing up is much easier than climbing down. You'll need to practice down climbing to feel competent when you need to do it. Reversing moves on a boulder problem instead of topping out or climbing up and then down the entire climb when on top rope rather than getting lowered by the rope are good ways to learn this skill.

### Ascending the rope

If, for some reason, you or your partner gets injured on a multi-pitch climb, you may need to ascend using the rope. To do this, you'll need to have with you an *ascender*, a device that slides

## WHEN YOU GET CAUGHT IN BAD WEATHER

Unlike gravity, which is always present, bad weather is one of the forces of nature that can catch you off guard. You can end up having to bail out, which is always a situation that has accident potential. There is no scarier sensation than walking across wet slabs of rock; what is totally casual when dry becomes a slippery-slide nightmare. As for climbing on wet rock, well, it's nearly impossible because of the lack of friction. If you are caught in a deluge, you also run into the problem of your ropes getting saturated, which makes them heavy, hard to manage, and weaker. Your best bet is to be prepared for the weather. Always pay attention to the weather forecasts, particularly if you're doing a long route or are climbing in a remote area. If the forecast sounds sketchy, choose a shorter climb—something you know you'll be able to retreat from safely if necessary. Be sure you know the weather patterns if you're climbing in a new area. Ask the local climbers for their recommendations. There are two types of climbing you can do if you must climb under the threat of rain: overhanging routes and indoor gym climbing.

"**T**here is some inherent risk . . . that's the distinction that separates climbing from other sports. I found that my attraction to climbing wasn't that risk per se, but instead it was my ability to create a reasonably safe experience in the mountains through good judgment and preparedness."

—Mattie Sheafor, Exum guide, founder of Women That Rock

freely up the rope but when weighted grabs and holds the rope (*ascenders* are mostly used in aid climbing but are also used for rescue). Aid climbers use mechanical ascenders specifically designed for this task; however, these are heavy, somewhat bulky devices not really designed for being taken along on free climbs. The most common ascenders that free climbers carry are either nylon cords (preferably 6- or 7-millimeter accessory cord) tied into slings about 2 to 3 feet long for tying *prusik knots* (see illustration page 153) on the rope, or a rope-grabbing device that serves the same purpose. Fortunately, there are now some emergency ascending devices on the market that are small and super light, such as the Petzl Tibloc. Once on the rope, these ascenders will slide up the rope freely, but when weighted they grab onto the rope.

The easiest way to ascend will be to use two prusiks or Tiblocs on the rope. Clip a sling into your harness with a locking carabiner, and attach the sling to the upper ascender either with a girth hitch or with another locking carabiner. Take another sling (or some quickdraws clipped together) and clip this into the lower ascender. This lower sling will act as a stirrup that you'll keep one foot in. For added safety, you'll also clip another sling that is attached to your harness into the lower ascender in case the upper one fails. To make upward progress, stand in the foot loop you've created hanging from the lower ascender. Then, with all your weight on this loop, slide the upper ascender up the rope (the one attached to your harness). Now you'll sit on this upper ascender so that your weight is off the

## THE DISTINCTION BETWEEN MOUNTAIN CLIMBERS AND ROCK CLIMBERS

Many people have the impression that mountain climbers and rock climbers are one and the same. I quite often am referred to as "Shelley, the mountain climber" by well-meaning but misinformed people. Once you're a climber, you'll find the same thing happening to you. There is a clear distinction, however, between the risk level of mountain climbing and that of rock climbing. The summits of the big mountains of the world are thrilling attractions for mountain climbers, but the objective dangers that mountain climbers must accept to reach these summits are far beyond what the average rock climber will ever encounter. Avalanches, altitude sickness, cerebral edema, hidden crevasses, bad weather, frostbite, and so on are some of the inherent risks of mountaineering. These risks are usually of the variety that the climber cannot control. The list of experienced mountain climbers who have been killed in the mountains is evidence of the unforgiving nature of these risks. More often than not, their deaths were not the result of errors they made but instead a result of the odds catching up with them. The more a climber goes into the mountains, the greater her chances are to have a run-in with one of these hazards.

By contrast, the list of experienced rock climbers being killed is a lot shorter. That isn't to say that there are no deaths, but the majority of deaths in rock climbing situations have been caused by human error, rather than by external, objective dangers like those in mountain climbing.

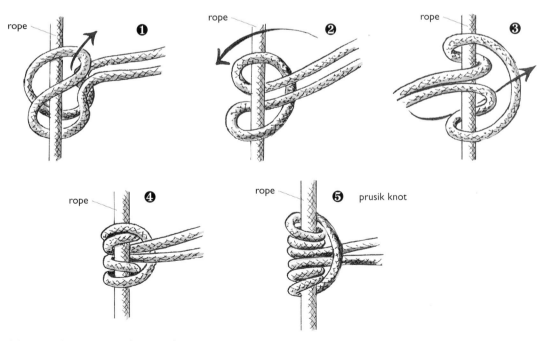

**Prusik knots** on the rope are used to ascend.

Tibloc

The **Tibloc** is a mini rope ascender that only weighs 39 grams. Carry prusiks or Tiblocs—they serve the save purpose.

lower one, which you'll then slide up. You'll then repeat the process: stand in the lower ascender to unweight the upper one so you can slide it up the rope; then sit on the upper one to unweight the lower one so you can slide it up, and so on.

## Retreating from a route

If you must retreat from a route because of bad weather or injury, you'll need to rappel or lower off. If the route is one that is set up for rappelling, you're in luck because it will already have fixed belay and rappel stations. If you need to leave your own gear behind, you'll need to be sure that you follow this advice. As stated above, don't ever rappel or lower off of just one piece of gear. Place at least two pieces and, if you or your partner is lowering rather than rappelling, be certain to run the rope through carabiners, not webbing.

### UNDERSTANDING FIRST AID

Climbing accidents are quite rare, but they do happen. Unfortunately, most climbers are woefully ignorant when it comes to first aid. Of course, all climbers should know the basics, such as how to stop bleeding, how to keep an unconscious person's air passages clear, and when not to move an injured person. Taking a first-aid course is a good idea; at the very least, pick up a book like *Self Rescue* (see chapter 10).

A smart climber would also carry a few essential items in her pack, in case of a small medical emergency. Here are some suggestions for first-aid preparedness.

- cloth athletic tape
- pocket knife (Swiss Army–type)
- antiseptic wipes
- antibacterial ointment
- Band-Aids
- self-adhering wrapping bandages for stabilizing sprains
- aspirin, acetaminophen, or ibuprofen

# Chapter 9

# NEXT STEPS: TAKING YOUR CLIMBING FURTHER

Where can you go in climbing? There are so many things you can do and places you can go. In this chapter, I explore some further adventures of the sport.

Up until now, I've focused a great deal of attention on the physical movement of climbing and the mental challenges you'll face in this sport. I've chosen this method because no other book I've seen for beginners teaches you these things. And because there are many texts written on the mechanics of the safety systems, placing protection, building anchors, equalizing the forces on the system—all the techniques the leading climber needs to know—I've chosen to give you information that isn't so easily found. In this chapter, however, I give you some tips on how to get started going out on your own.

> Leading for the first time is the most exciting, rewarding, scary, and challenging thing you can imagine.

## LEAD CLIMBING

At some stage, you're going to want to go beyond having everything always set up for you as it is in the gym or with the guide or instructor. You're going to want to take charge of your own climbing. The combination of placing your own gear, finding your own way, setting up your own anchors, and

**Above:** Sport climbing at Devil's Punchbowl, California.
**Below:** The climber's rope must go up through the back of the carabiner (the side closest to the rock) and come out the front, exiting the carabiner away from the rock as shown in **A**. If the climber clips into the carabiner incorrectly (the rope goes into the front of the biner and comes out the back), the rope could potentially run across the gate and unclip itself (**B**).

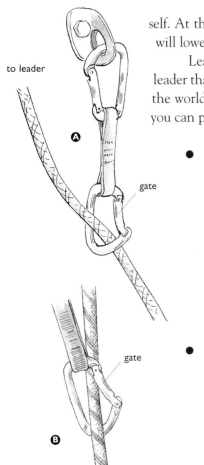

even taking your own leader falls is what most climbers feel makes the ultimate climbing experience. Leading for the first time is the most exciting, rewarding, scary, and challenging thing you can imagine. I highly recommend it. So, how do you learn to lead climb? Here are my tips.

### Leading sport routes

In sport climbing, the leader doesn't have to place her own protection; she simply carries a rack of quickdraws and clips them onto the preplaced bolts. Then, like all leading, she clips her rope into the bottom carabiner of the draw. Once she gets to the end of the route, the anchor is also already fixed there, so she needs only to clip into it to safety herself. At that point, she doesn't even need to set up a belay because her belayer will lower her to the ground from that point.

Learning to lead on a sport climb is certainly less demanding of the new leader than learning to lead with gear. I recommend this as your first foray into the world of leading; it's certainly the least intimidating. Here are some ways you can prepare for leading your first sport route.

- **Practice clipping the rope into a quickdraw.** One of the hardest things for any climber is figuring out how to clip into the carabiners on the quickdraws. (See the drawing for correct and incorrect clipping.). The rope must *always* be clipped correctly, or the climber runs the risk of the rope unclipping itself—a very disconcerting possibility. The best way to learn how to clip is to practice by setting up a couple of quickdraws at the base of a gym route or even at home from a coat rack so you can stand on the ground and repeatedly clip the draws until it comes naturally.

- **Practice leading on top rope.** With a top rope belay, tie into another rope and pretend to lead on that line. This will help you get the feel of handling the rope for clipping in. If you do this outside, you should even put your own quickdraws on the bolts. (Gym routes usually have fixed quickdraws in place.) This practice leading technique is how many gyms will have you begin leading. I think it's a great thing to do at least twice before taking off for real.

• • • • • • • • • • • • • • • • • • • • • • • • • • • • • • • • • • • • • • •

**U**se every experience following and cleaning a gear route to learn about how it all works.

• • • • • • • • • • • • • • • • • • • • • • • • • • • • • • • • • • • • • • •

## Lead climbing on traditional routes

Certainly there is much more involved in leading a trad or gear route. On this subject alone I could write an entire book. And many books *have* been written that include whole chapters dedicated to the nuts and bolts of lead climbing with natural protection (see chapter 10). Almost everyone begins their (trad) lead climbing apprenticeship by following many trad routes first. In fact, with the exception of the first couple of times out climbing, you should use every experience following and cleaning a gear route to learn about how it all works. Climb with an experienced trad climber, and keep a keen eye on all she does. As you remove protection points she's placed, analyze how they went into the rock and why they work. You can even remove and replace them so that you begin to get the feel of a good placement. When you arrive at the belay anchors, don't just clip in and ignore the handiwork of the

Placing gear on lead, Escalante Canyon, Colorado.

leader. Take a good look at the anchor system she's built, and ask her to explain what she's done and to show you why it works. Every anchor is different; the more examples you see, the better prepared you'll be to do it on your own.

You can also practice placing gear without leaving the ground. Wander along the base of cliffs or boulders looking for cracks to place pro. You can even set up mock anchors this way. To be sure you're setting solid placements, have an experienced partner check it for you. And just as I explained above, a trial run with a top rope for your first venture into leading with gear is a great way to get the hang of it without risking taking your first leader fall.

The art and science of placing pro and setting up anchors is serious business, and learning how to do it requires practical experience. To get this experience, I suggest you take a class or get an experienced climbing friend to teach you. There are also a couple of good books I recommend in chapter 10 (*Climbing Anchors* and *More Climbing Anchors*) that can complement your practical instruction. However, again I don't recommend trying to learn solely from a book.

## COMPETITION CLIMBING

In my early years in the sport, I was so incredibly self-conscious about climbing around a lot of people that I never imagined I would compete. In fact, back then, competitions and sport climb-

Climbing in local competitions can be a way to help you develop confidence, but there are competitions all the way up to international levels. Here, Elena Ovchinnikova is on the final route at the X Games, San Diego, California.

ing didn't even exist, and they wouldn't for years to come. I had initially pursued climbing because it was outside the realm of organized sports, which I believed was something only *real* athletes could participate in (I didn't think I was one of them). The truth was, when I began competing I didn't have very much confidence in myself, nor did I consider myself a competitive type. I very nearly convinced myself that I wouldn't be any good at it, so I shouldn't even bother. The reason I'm writing this section is that I'm so glad that I did do it!

By participating in competition climbing, I learned more about myself as a climber, I became stronger than I ever imagined I could be, and I learned how to set goals, how to train, and how to be focused and relaxed on command. It taught me so many wonderful things that not only have helped me in my everyday climbing, but also have helped me succeed in a competitive world.

There are many levels of competition in climbing: the just-for-fun local events at the gym, the party atmosphere events like the Phoenix Bouldering Competition held on natural rock outside of Phoenix, the regional and national events sanctioned by the American Sport Climbing Federation with points that count toward the national ranking. Then there are the big international events, such as the World Cup circuit, the X Games, and the most prestigious invitational of all: the Rock Master, which is held in Arco, Italy. Certainly, to start out, you'll want to try a local or even regional event. They usually have categories ranging from beginner to expert or elite, and the field is divided into men's and women's classes. The gym or the organizer of the event will be able to help you figure out what category is best for you.

Once you've signed up, you automatically have a goal and a time frame for achieving that goal. It's an opportunity for you to really push yourself and to discover your strengths and weaknesses. Plus, you'll get the chance to meet other women like yourself. You'll be surprised by the camaraderie that develops among women at competitions because you're all experiencing the same fears, the same performance anxieties, and the same precompetition jitters. We have so much to learn from one another. I met some of my best friends and climbing partners at competitions.

**W**e have so much to learn from one another. I met some of my best friends and climbing partners at competitions.

## CLIMBING HOLIDAYS

The world is full of wonderful places for climbing. And the great thing about climbing areas, particularly destination crags, is that they're nearly always located in some beautiful, and sometimes exotic, place. It's not hard to find out where these destination crags are. Nearly every issue of the climbing magazines contains at least one article on some destination. The articles often include directions for getting there, the best time of year to go, mini-guidebooks or excerpts of topos from the guidebook for the area, recommended climbs, and lodging options. You can also just ask around. Climbing is a very small world, and climbers love to share their travel experiences. When you've narrowed your choices, here are some things to consider before you book a ticket or pack the car.

Multi-pitch limestone climbing in Buoux, France.

- **Can I go to this area alone, or do I need to travel with a partner?**
  At some areas, you can show up without a climbing partner and readily find other climbers seeking partners. Usually, the search for a partner is facilitated by some sort of communal *hang*: a climber's campground, a café or restaurant where everyone gathers, or even the cliff area itself as a social gathering place. This is true of areas such as Joshua Tree, Yosemite, the Red River Gorge, Smith Rocks, Rifle, and even Phra Nang in Thailand and Mt. Arapiles in Australia.

  The main problems with this strategy include the possibility that some days you may not find a partner and that, unless you have the experience to judge someone's competency as a climber, you may end up with someone who isn't safe (see page 146). Be aware of the climbing areas where you are unlikely to find a partner. If the cliff has a long approach or if the crags are very isolated, such as the Calanques in France or the Blue Mountains in Australia, or if the area is known for its long and committing routes, such as those in the Dolomites in Italy or Long's Peak in Colorado, you won't be able to just show

*(continued page 162)*

# POPULAR DESTINATION CLIMBING AREAS

Here are some of my picks for a climbing holiday. I chose these sites based on personal experience or recommendations from climbing friends. Keep in mind that these are just a select few of the favorite areas; there are many other options throughout the world that I didn't have room to include. If you're keen to go to a certain country or certain region, ask around among climbing acquaintances, browse the book section of an outdoor store, or read back issues of the climbing magazines to find out what the climbing is like there.

## United States

**Joshua Tree, California.** A great area for escaping the winter blues. Located just east of Los Angeles, "J Tree" is a wonderland of many enormous boulders and rounded outcrops of rock formations in the desert. Most of the routes are single pitch traditional climbs of both the crack and face climbing variety. The camping and the climbing are very communal and it offers a very social atmosphere. Not much in the way of nightlife in the small town of Joshua Tree or Twenty-nine Palms, but the hiking and running trails are great.

**Yosemite National Park and Tuolumne Meadows, California.** In the sixties and seventies, Yosemite was considered the center of the climbing universe. It still is the most incredible place for traditional crack climbing on granite. There are routes of every grade from single-pitch to multi-pitch. The best seasons to go are spring and fall. If you plan a trip in the summer, head up to Tuolumne Meadows, which is at a much higher elevation although still part of Yosemite National Park. The routes offer more face climbing, and the weather is stellar during the summer. When you're not climbing, the hiking, backpacking, and magnificent scenery will keep you busy.

**Rifle, Colorado.** Rifle is considered *the* sport climbing crag in the United States. The limestone rock at this area is the closest imitation we have of European-type limestone (very featured, yet pretty solid). It's also got easy access, pleasant camping, and lots of climbers looking for partners. The main drawback is that there aren't many easy graded routes. You should be climbing at least easy 5.11 to get the most out of the area. The season is late spring through late fall. For activities other than climbing, visit Glenwood Springs with its famous hot springs (about 45 minutes away) and Aspen for a taste of mountain high society (about an hour and a half away).

**Red River Gorge, Kentucky.** Located about an hour from Lexington, Kentucky, "The Red" is one of the best climbing areas in the country. The area has several cliffs of mostly single-pitch sport climbs on the most unusual type of sandstone I've ever encountered. Unlike most sandstone areas, it seems that there are holds everywhere, because the rock is so featured and textured. There isn't a great deal to do in the area aside from climbing, other than the tourist attractions Cincinnati, Louisville, and Lexington offer (all within a couple of hours drive). Still, it is certainly one of my top picks in the eastern part of the country to take a climbing vacation.

**Red Rocks, Las Vegas, Nevada.** From October until April, the warm weather and sunshine makes the Red Rocks the favorite winter destination for climbers from all over the world. Airfare can be quite cheap and some trip bargains even include lodging packages. There are hundreds of routes of both the trad and sport climbing variety. You can choose multi-pitch routes or single-pitch climbs with plenty of opportunity for lying on the rocks, soaking up the sun. Of course, the Vegas Strip offers a unique distraction for rest days or evenings.

**Smith Rocks, Oregon.** Located near Bend, Oregon, this area was one of the first "sport climbing" areas developed in the United States. It has a fair number of great traditional climbs, as well. The best thing about Smith Rocks is that the area is so concentrated: you can do a lot of climbing without a lot of walking from climb to climb. The season is pretty long there; from March through May and then September through November are the ideal months for good climbing weather. Portland is a couple of hours to the north if you want to find great restaurants and coffeehouses on your days off.

**New River Gorge, West Virginia.** One of the most extensive areas in the East, "The New" is popular because of its high-quality sandstone climbing. Most of the climbs are single-pitch, but there are hundreds of them. And the sport climber will be as happy as the traditional climber, as there are both crack climbs and bolted face climbs side by side. The weather can be humid and rainy in summer, so spring and fall are best.

French national champion Liz Sansoz, enjoying her vacation in Rifle, Colorado.

## Elsewhere in the World

**South of France.** This is a truly amazing place for a climbing holiday. The south of France has been bestowed with an extraordinarily high concentration of limestone cliffs, and the French have developed them into premier sport climbing crags. You can base yourself in the region of Aix-en-Provence and visit many different crags within a two-hour driving radius. You won't find traditional crack climbs because of the characteristics of the limestone. However, face climbing here doesn't get any better. The crags themselves are tourist attractions, but the nonclimbing attractions are abundant as well: beaches along the Mediterranean, quaint old villages throughout Provence, the cities of Avignon, Nice, Monaco, and Marseilles—and, of course, the food and wine are always worth indulging in. Best times to go are spring and fall.

**Italy.** There are many areas to climb throughout Italy, although most traveling climbers head to Northern Italy. The area around Lago di Garda is one of the most famous and popular because of the many different crags located in the region. The nearby town of Arco hosts the celebrated Rock Master's climbing competition every September, where the best climbers in the world come to compete. As in most of Europe, the rock is limestone. The weather is best in spring and fall, although it's possible to climb there in the summer. There are lakes for swimming or windsurfing, the countryside is gorgeous and the food is fantastic. You can also journey up to the Dolomites and climb some of the pre-equipped Via Ferrata routes (long, mountain routes set up with steel cables and ladders to make the ascents to the summits safe and accessible, even for nontechnical climbers and hikers).

**El Portrero Chico, Mexico.** Located in northeastern Mexico, about an hour-and-a-half drive from Monterey, this recently developed limestone area is an inexpensive, winter destination. It's a sport climbing area with routes of every length starting at 5.8 or 5.9. Unlike most sport climbing areas, El Portrero has many excellent multi-pitch routes as well as plenty of single-pitch routes. In addition to high-quality routes, you'll find that the cost of a climbing holiday is quite low. The camping is outfitted with hot showers and stoves for cooking and is located within walking distance of the cliffs. For a little more, you can rent a *casita* (cottage) in the same area. During the peak (winter) holiday periods, you could go to El Portrero without a partner and find plenty of people to climb with. There are also mountain biking trails and a hot springs retreat in the vicinity.

*(continued next page)*

## POPULAR DESTINATION CLIMBING AREAS *(continued from previous page)*

**Spain.** Like France, Spain has been blessed with plenty of limestone cliffs. The climate is quite a bit warmer, so the season for enjoyable weather is longer. The style of the climbing is similar to France, but with far fewer people. The greatest concentration of climbing areas is along Spain's eastern coast, with Barcelona a great place to start. There is even a fantastic climbing destination on the Spanish island of Mallorca, located just off the coast of Barcelona (about 45 minutes by air). Rest days can be spent basking on the beaches of the Mediterranean or visiting the fantastic sites in Barcelona or the smaller towns.

**Thailand.** For an exotic climbing getaway, Thailand tops the list. The crags, Phra Nang and Railay Beach, are located near a town called Krabi in the south of Thailand. The entire area is covered with towering cliffs of limestone and dense unspoiled jungle, which conceal fantastic caves full of stalactites and stalagmites. With white beaches against an aquamarine sea bordering the cliffs, you couldn't ask for a more picture-picture holiday. The peninsula on which Phra Nang and Railay Beach are situated juts out from the mainland and is only accessible by boat. There are very inexpensive bungalows for rent near the climbing areas. And in the peak holiday season (December and January), you'll have no problem finding climbing partners, should you journey solo. The dry season is short one, from October to January.

*(continued from page 159)*

up and find a willing partner. You also probably won't find someone easily in any European country where climbing tourists are ubiquitous. You may find fellow travelers who are in the same situation as you are. However, the local climber's openness and willingness to befriend strangers is a rare occurrence.

- **What's the weather *really* like there at that time of year?** During my first trip to the south of France, I froze my butt off. I'd heard only the travel brochure version of the fall weather there, which sounded warm and balmy. Be sure to ask someone who's been there at the time of year you plan to go to get the full picture. Also, be prepared to do some sightseeing and touristy activities because invariably you will have some bad weather.

- **Should I hire a guide or go it on my own?** This will depend on how independent you are as a climber, of course. You may want to hire a guide initially, even if you feel competent as a climber, just to get a feel for the place (the approaches, the descents, the best routes, the best restaurants, and so on). If you do go it on your own, you'll definitely want to buy a guidebook in advance if you can. Many good outdoor shops carry a selection of guidebooks for the popular destinations. If they don't have the book you want, ask them whether they can special order it for you. Guidebooks are invaluable for the visiting climber.

● **How can I prepare for the climbing?** Some people go on a climbing trip and don't have as much fun as they could have because they didn't realize how different the rock might be or they weren't physically fit enough to enjoy the routes. Prepare for your trip by finding out the nature of the rock and training for it in the gym. Also, be sure to find out by reading the guidebook whether there is any special gear you'll need to bring, so you don't have to seek out a climbing shop in an unfamiliar city before you can get on the rocks.

## CLIMBING WITH KIDS

Children are the most natural climbers in the world. In fact, they'll probably out-climb you most of the time unless they simply can't reach the holds. Kids have an amazing strength-to-body-weight ratio, which is precisely what's needed for climbing. The earliest age to introduce kids to climbing is around three or four years old. Before that, they don't yet have the attention span or the physical coordination for it. The ideal ages are five

Adults can pick up many tips on technique from their kids. At 7 years old, Krystal Sagan climbed with more natural talent and technique than anyone else at the gym that day.

## TIPS FOR CLIMBING WITH KIDS

- If climbing outdoors, put plenty of sunscreen on exposed skin.

- Bring lots of food, juice, and water for kids to snack and drink throughout the day.

- Depending on the child's age, you may also want to bring other distractions such as toys, games, or paper and crayons, since kids may get bored with climbing or waiting for you to climb.

- Always have children wear helmets, even when not climbing.

- Monitor children closely to ensure that those who aren't climbing stay clear of the base of the cliff and away from boulders where adults are climbing. Even a climber on a rope could fall and end up very near to the children.

- Don't force children to climb if they decide they don't want to. Pushing them or teasing them into climbing will only instill fears and inhibitions about the sport.

- The relatively safe and nonintimidating atmosphere of a climbing gym is usually the best venue for introducing children to the sport.

Indoor climbing gyms can allow a reasonably controlled, good introduction to the sport for children.

• • • • • • • • • • • • • • • • • • • • • • • • • •

Children are the most natural climbers in the world.

• • • • • • • • • • • • • • • • • • • • • • • • • •

to seven because they can really grasp the concepts, they are becoming more coordinated, and they are still young enough to not have any preconceived notions about what is and isn't possible.

Kids do great at both indoor and outdoor climbing, although indoor climbing is somewhat less intimidating. Always have your kids wearing helmets outside whether they're just bouldering or they're top roping. They should be taught to always be aware of who is climbing above them; this is especially true in a bouldering situation, where adult climbers might be falling off boulder problems out of control. Even a helmet wouldn't do much good if a 180-pound adult landed on top of a six-year-old.

For younger children, a full-body harness is the only way to go. Up to a certain age, a kid's center of gravity is much higher than an adult's; this makes the kid top-heavy and more inclined to flip upside down when she falls. A full-body harness will prevent this. Kids probably shouldn't learn to belay until they get to an age at which they can understand the seriousness of the task. Most gyms set the minimum age for belaying at 11 to 13. I'd be very cautious about letting a very light child belay an adult—even if the child is anchored to the ground. Be sure that when teaching a child to belay, she gets a chance to hold plenty of practice falls. I also recommend having the child belay with a Grigri; it will back her up should anything go wrong.

Make sure that all of the child's experiences are on fairly easy climbs, so that she's always having fun. Once a child gets to an age where she is conscious of the grades, your only concern should be that she doesn't get too hung up on the ratings of the climbs. The unfortunate truth is that even though kids are 20 times stronger than the adults around them are, their short stature will at times hinder them or even prevent them from doing certain routes.

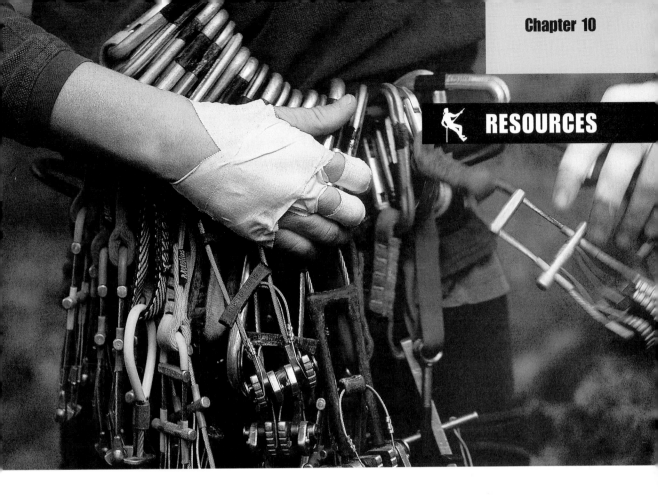

# Chapter 10

# RESOURCES

F or all of your initial investigation, I highly recommend starting your search on the Internet. Although I'm personally familiar with several guide services, gyms, and climbing shops (particularly those in the west), I did a lot of browsing on the web to see what else was available for readers in other parts of the country. It's astounding how many sites exist that offer information or links to just about anything a climber or aspiring climber could want. Just go to your favorite search engine and plug in "climbing" plus gyms, guide services, or whatever you seek. I've included URLs for several sites I visited. However, the list is far from exhaustive, and I highly recommend just surfing on your own.

## BOOKS

### More climbing knowledge

Bensman, Bobbi. *Bouldering with Bobbi Bensman*. Mechanicsburg PA: Stackpole Books, 1999.

Bigon, Mario, and Guido Regazzoni. *The Morrow Guide to Knots*. Milan, Italy: William Morrow, 1981.

Cinnamon, Jerry. *The Complete Climber's Handbook*. Camden ME: Ragged Mountain Press, 2000.

Erbesfield, Robyn, and Steve Boga. *Sport Climbing with Robyn Erbesfield*. Mechanicsburg PA: Stackpole Books, 1997.

Lewis, S. Peter. *Top Roping*.

Helena MT: Falcon Press, 1998.

Long, John. *Climbing Anchors*. Mechanicsburg PA: Stackpole Books, 1998.

Long, John. *How to Rock Climb!*, 3rd ed. Helena MT: Chockstone Press, 1999.

Long, John, and Bob Gaines. *More Climbing Anchors: How*

*to Rock Climb.* Helena MT: Chockstone Press, 1998.

Loughman, Michael. *Learning to Rock Climb.* San Francisco: Sierra Club Books, 1981.

Luebben, Craig. *How to Climb: Rappelling.* Helena MT: Falcon Press, forthcoming.

Prichard, Nancy. *The I Hate to Train Performance Guide for Climbers.* Evergreen CO: Chockstone Press, 1994.

Raleigh, Duane. *Knots and Ropes for Climbers.* Mechanicsburg PA: Stackpole Books, 1998.

### First aid and rescue

Fasulo, David. *Self Rescue.* Helena MT: Falcon Press, 1999.

Gill, Paul G. *The Ragged Mountain Press Pocket Guide to Wilderness Medicine and First Aid.* Camden ME: Ragged Mountain Press, 1997.

Preston, Gilbert. *Wilderness First Aid: When You Can't Call 911.* Helena MT: Falcon Press, 1997.

### Honing the mind

Al Huang, Chungliang, and Jerry Lynch. *Thinking Body, Dancing Mind: Tao Sports for Extraordinary Performance in Athletics, Business and Life.* New York: Bantam, 1992.

Loehr, James E. *Mental Toughness Training for Sports.* Lexington MA: S. Greene Press, 1986.

Orlick, Terry. *Psyching for Sport: Mental Training for Athletes.* Champaign IL: Leisure Press, 1986.

Ungerleider, Steven. *Mental Training for Peak Performance: Top Athletes Reveal the Mind Exercises They Use to Excel.* Emmaus PA: Rodale Press, 1996.

## MAGAZINES

*Climbing Magazine*
0326 Highway 133, Suite 190
Carbondale CO 81623
970-963-9449, 800-493-4569
Fax 970-963-9442
E-mail: climbing@climbing.com
www.climbing.com

*Rock and Ice*
603 South Broadway, Suite A
Boulder CO 80303
303-499-8410, 877-ROCKICE
   (877-762-5423)
Fax 303-499-4131
E-mail: editor@rockandice. com
www.rockandice.com

## WEBSITES

www.mountainwoman.com
www.climbarock.com
www.adventuresports.com
www.rockandgroove.com
www.climbnet.com
www.mountainzone.com
www.rocklist.com

## SCHOOLS AND GUIDE SERVICES

**Exum Mountain Guides**
Grand Teton National Park WY
307-733-2297

**First Ascent Climbing Services, Inc.**
1136 SW Deschutes
Redmond OR 97756

541-548-5137, 800-325-5462
Fax 541-548-3175
E-mail: ascent@goclimbing.com
www.goclimbing.com

**Women That Rock**
P.O. Box 1467
Jackson WY 83001
307-733-8347
E-mail:
   info@womenthatrock.com
www.womenthatrock.com

## CLUBS AND ASSOCIATIONS

**Access Fund**
P.O. Box 17010
Boulder CO 80308
303-545-6772
Fax 303-545-6774
www.outdoorlink.com/access-fund/

**American Alpine Club**
710 Tenth St., Suite 100
Golden CO 80401
303-384-0110
Fax 303-384-0111
www.americanalpineclub.org

**American Mountain Guide Association**
710 Tenth St., Suite 101
Golden CO 80401
303-271-0984
Fax 303-271-1377
E-mail: info@amga.com
www.amga.com

**American Sport Climbing Federation (ASCF)**
710 Tenth St., Suite 130
Golden CO 80401
888-ASCF-ROX (888-272-3769)
International: 970-586-5303
www.mindspring.com/~ascf/

## WOMEN'S CLIMBING APPAREL

**Stonewear Designs**
4699 Nautilus Court S., Suite 504
Boulder CO 80301
303-530-3035, 800-860-3653
Fax 303-530-3065
E-mail: stonewr@trango.com
www.stoneweardesigns.com

**Verve**
1081 11th St.
Boulder CO 80302
303-443-7010
Fax 303-545-9558
E-mail: cgverve@aol.com

## CLIMBING GYMS

This state-by-state list—with Canada at the end—has gyms alphabetized under municipalities in that state. The list is not complete, so if you don't see a gym listed for your area, check the phone book or check with your local outdoors store to find out where the closest climbing gym is.

## Alabama

**Gold's Gym of Auburn**
Auburn AL
205-821-3600

**Alabama Outdoors**
Birmingham AL
800-870-0011

**Jugheads**
Birmingham AL
205-945-1966

**Rock Town Indoor
  Climbing Gym**
Birmingham AL
205-945-9010

**Vertical Reality Sport
  Climbing Gym**
Huntsville AL
205-880-0770

**Sports Xtreme Inc**
Mobile AL
334-639-0099

## Alaska

**Alaska Rock Gym**
Anchorage AK
907-562-7265
www.alaskan.com/akrockgym

**Cassel Rock**
Anchorage AK
907-563-3041

**Moseley Sports Center**
Anchorage AK
907-564-8354

**Rock of Ages Climbing Gym**
Wasilla AK
907-376-4966

## Arizona

**Vertical Relief Climbing
  Center**
Flagstaff AZ
520-556-9909

**Arizona Climbing Center**
Phoenix AZ
602-997-4171

**Prescott YMCA Climbing
  Wall**
Prescott AZ
520-445-7221

**Climb Max**
Tempe AZ

**Phoenix Rock Gym**
Tempe AZ
602-921-8322

**Rocks and Ropes
  Climbing Gym**
Tucson AZ
602-882-5924
www.rocksandropes.com

## Arkansas

**Fayetteville Rock Gym**
Fayetteville AR
501-442-6526

**La Casa Pollo Sport
  Climbing Facility**
Fayetteville AR
501-444-6132

**Fitness F-X**
Little Rock AR
501-221-0720

## California

**Alpine Experience**
Anaheim Hills CA
714-777-4884

**Rocktopia**
Concord CA
510-938-7625

**Rockreation Climbing Center**
Costa Mesa CA
714-556-ROCK (714-556-7625)
www.rockreation.com

**Rocknasium**
Davis CA
530-757-2902
www.wworks.com/~rockgym

**Cityrock**
Emeryville CA
510-654-2510
www.cityrock.com

**Rock Climb**
Fresno CA
209-448-0643

**Ascent Climbing Gym**
Grass Valley CA
916-272-0170

**Climb X**
Huntington Beach CA
714-843-9919

**Sporting Club**
Irvine CA
714-250-4422

**Power House Gym**
Livermore CA
510-449-3539

**Sunrise Rock Gym**
Livermore CA
925-447-8003

**Loma Linda University**
Loma Linda CA
714-824-4975

**CornerStone**
Long Beach CA
213-493-4999

**The Rock Gym**
Long Beach CA
562-983-5500
therockgym.home.mindspring.
  com

**L.A. Rock Gym**
Los Angeles CA
310-973-3388
www.flash.net/~cfoster2/la_rock/

**Quantum Rock**
Los Angeles CA
310-378-2171

**Rockreation Climbing Center**
Los Angeles CA
310-207-7199
www.rockreation.com

**Arete Rock Climbing Park**
Los Gatos CA

**Stonehenge Climbing Gym**
Modesto CA
209-521-3644

**Twisters**
Mountain View CA
650-969-1636

**Rock and Roll**
Murrieta CA
714-677-7439

**Headwall Cafe and Climbing**
Olympic Valley CA
916-583-7673

**Uprising**
Palm Springs CA
760-320-6630, 888-CLIMB-ON
  (888-254-6266)
www.uprising.com

**Climb USA**
Placerville CA
916-662-3222

**Solid Rock Gym**
Poway CA
619-299-1124
www.solidrockgym.com

**Granite Arch**
Rancho Cordova CA
916-852-7625
www.granitearch.com

**Sanctuary Rock Gym**
Sand City CA
831-899-2595
www.rockgym.com

**Solid Rock Gym**
San Diego CA
619-299-1124
www.solidrockgym.com

**Vertical HoldSport Climbing
  Center**
San Diego CA

619-586-7572
www.verticalhold.com

**Mission Cliffs**
San Francisco CA
415-550-0515
www.mission-cliffs.com

**Crux Climbing Gym**
San Luis Obispo CA
805-544-8203

**Class 5**
San Rafael CA
415-485-6931
www.class5.com

**UC Santa Barbara Gym**
Santa Barbara CA
805-893-3737

**Planet Granite**
Santa Clara CA
408-727-2777
www.planetgranite.com

**Pacific Edge**
Santa Cruz CA
831-454-9254
www.pacclimb.com

**Vertex**
Santa Rosa CA
707-573-1608

**Gad Gym**
South Lake Tahoe CA
916-544-7314

**Gravity Works**
Truckee CA
916-582-4510

**NorthStar Climbing Wall**
Truckee CA
702-856-4824

**Hanger 18 Indoor Climbing Gym**
Upland CA
909-931-5991

## Colorado

**Aspen Athletic Club**
Aspen CO
303-925-2531

**Boulder Rock Club**
Boulder CO
303-447-2804
www.boulderrock.com

**CATS**
Boulder CO
303-939-9699

**Breckenridge Recreation Center**
Breckenridge CO
303-453-1734

**Holubar**
Colorado Springs CO
303-453-0626

**Sport Climbing Club**
Colorado Springs CO
303-447-2804

**US Sport Climbing Center of Colorado Springs**
Colorado Springs CO
719-578-5555

**Colorado Indoor**
Denver CO
303-680-9441

**Colorado Outdoor**
Denver CO
303-825-8168

**Paradise Rock Gym**
Denver CO
303-286-8168

**Thrillseekers**
Denver CO
303-733-8810

**Animas City Rock**
Durango CO

970-259-5700
www.climbacr.com

**Healthworks**
Fort Collins CO
303-493-2101

**Inner Strength**
Fort Collins CO
970-282-8118

**Glenwood Springs Climbing Gym**
Glenwood Springs CO
970-945-7898

**Rock of Ages Climbery**
Grand Junction CO
970-945-7898

**Vertical Works Climbing Gym**
Grand Junction CO
303-245-3610

**The Point Athletic**
Lakewood CO
303-988-1300

**Steamboat Athletic Club**
Steamboat Springs CO
303-879-1036

**Vertical Grip**
Steamboat Spings CO
970-879-5421

**A. K. Rock Gym**
Summit County CO

**ROCK'n & JAM'n**
Thornton CO
303-CLIMB-99 (303-254-6299)

**Vail Athletic Club**
Vail CO
303-476-0700

**Westminster Climbing Wall**
Westminster CO
303-460-9690

## Connecticut

**Cliffs**
Danbury CT

**Ragged Mountain Outdoor Center**
Manchester CT
203-645-0015

**Stone Age Rock Gym**
Manchester CT

**Go Vertical Indoor Rock Climbing**
Stamford CT
203-358-8767
www.govertical.com

**Prime Climb Rock Gym**
Wallingford CT
203-265-7880
www.ezlink.com/~prime

## Delaware

**University of Delaware**
Newark DE

## Florida

**Coral Cliffs**
Fort Lauderdale FL
954-321-9898

**Peak Performers Climbing Gym**
Jacksonville FL
904-938-9808
www.peakperformers.com

**Aiguille Climbing Center**
Longwood FL
407-332-1430
www.aiguille.com

**X-Treme**
Miami FL
305-233-6623

**Weatherford's Climbing Wall**
Pensacola FL
904-469-9922

**On The Rocks**
Riviera Beach FL
561-842-2999

**Tallahassee Rock Gym**
Tallahassee FL
904-224-ROCK (904-224-7625)

**Vertical Ventures**
Tampa FL
813-884-ROCK (813-884-7625)
www.verticalventures.com

## Georgia

**Sporting Club at Windy Hill**
Atlanta GA
404-953-1100

**The Climb'n Shop**
Carrollton GA
404-834-2100

**Atlanta Rocks**
Doraville GA
770-242-ROCK (770-242-7625)
www.atlantarocks.com

**The Crux Climbing Center**
Columbus GA
706-324-6366

## Illinois

**Vertical Reality**
Aurora IL
630-892-1109

**RockAway Climbing Gym:**
Batavia IL
708-879-3636

**Upper Limits Climbing Gym**
Bloomington IL
309-829-8255
www.upperlimits.com

**Vertical Plains**
Champaign IL

**Lakeshore Athletic Club**
Chicago IL 60601
312-616-9000
www.corporateclimb.com

**North Wall Climbing Gym**
Crystal Lake IL
815-356-6855
E-mail: ookmuk@mc.net
www.user.mc.net/~ookmuk

**Climb On**
Homewood IL

**Indoor Summits**
Naperville IL

**GAR Indoor Climbing Gym**
Rockford IL

## Indiana

**Hoosier Heights Indoor
   Climbing**
Bloomington IN

**Climb Time**
Castleton IN

## Iowa

**Quad Cities Rock Gym**
Bettendorf IA

**B&B Mountaineering**
Kelley IA
515-769-2250
E-mail: mountain@pcpartner.net
www.midiowa.com/
   bb_mountaineering

## Louisiana

**Roc Haus**
Lafayette LA
318-981-8116
www.spydergrrls.com/rokhaus

**Climb Max**
New Orleans LA
504-486-7600
www.climb-max.com

## Maine

**Atlantic Climbing School**
P.O. Box 6003
Bar Harbor ME 04609
207-288-2521
www.acsclimb.com

**Maine Rock Gym**
127 Marginal Way
Portland ME 04101
207-780-6370
www.mainerockgym.com

**Unity College**
HC 78, Box 1
Unity ME 04998
207-948-3131, ext. 273
www.unity.edu

## Massachussetts

**Carabiner's Indoor Climbing**
New Bedford MA
508-677-0696
www.carabiners.com

## Maryland

**Earth Treks Climbing Center**
Columbia MD
410-872-0060
www.earthtreksclimbing.com

**The Hangout**
Finksburg MD

**Sport Rock Climbing Center**
Rockville MD
301-ROCK-111
   (301-702-5111)
www.sportrock.com

## Michigan

**Higher Ground Climbing Centre**
Grand Rapids MI

**Inside Moves**
Grand Rapids MI

**Climb Kalamazoo**
Kalamazoo MI

**Far Reach Climbing Gym**
Ottawa Lake MI

**Planet Rock**
Pontiac MI
248-334-3904

## Minnesota

**Footprints Climbing Gym**
Bloomington MN

**Rock Works Climbing Gym**
Minneapolis MN

**Vertical Endeavors**
St. Paul MN

## Missouri

**IBEX Rock Gym**
Blue Springs MO
816-228-9988

**Monster Mountain Gym**
Blue Springs MO

**Petra Rock Climbing Gym**
Springfield MO

## Nevada

**Powerhouse Climbing Gym**
Las Vegas NV
702-254-5604

**Vegas Rock Gym**
Las Vegas NV
702-434-3388

**RockSport Indoor Climbing Center**
Reno NV
775-358-4824
www.mountaineering.com/
   rocksport

## New Jersey

**Vertical Reality**
Cherry Hill NJ
609-273-1370

**Wall Street Rock Gym**
Edison NJ
908-412-1255

**New Jersey Rock Gym**
Wayne NJ
973-305-6777

**Up the Wall**
Wayne NJ
732-249-6422

## New York

**Chelsea Piers Sports Center Rock Wall**
New York NY
212-336-6083

## North Carolina

**Charlotte Climbing Center**
Charlotte NC
704-372-2382

**Inner Peaks Climbing Center**
Charlotte NC
704-588-6677
www.innerpeaks.com

**Vertical Edge Climbing Center**
East Durham NC
919-596-6910
www.vertical-edge.virtualave.net

**The Climbing Place**
Fayetteville NC

## Ohio

**Urban Krag**
Dayton OH
937-224-KRAG
   (937-224-5724)
E-mail: info@urbankrag.com
www.urbankrag.com

## Oklahoma

**OKC Rocks Indoor Climbing Gym**
Oklahoma City OK
www.okcrocks.com

**Tinker Air Force Base**
Oklahoma City OK
405-734-3162

**New Heights Rock Gym**
Tulsa OK

## Oregon

**Inclimb**
Bend OR
541-388-6764
E-mail: inclimb@cmpnet.com
www.inclimb.com

**The Crux Rock Gym**
Eugene OR
541-484-9535
E-mail: climb@cruxrock.com

## Pennsylvania

**Vertical Extreme**
Downingtown PA
610-873-9620

**Philadelphia Rock Gym**
Oaks PA
610-666-ROPE (610-666-7673)
www.philarockgym.com

**The Climbing Wall**
Pittsburgh PA
412-247-7334

**North Summit Climbing Gym**
Wind Gap PA
610-863-4444

## Texas

**Dyno-Rock Indoor
   Climbing Gym**
Arlington TX
817-461-3966
www.dynorock.com

**Austin Rock Gym**
Austin TX
512-416-9299
www.austinrockgym.com

**Exposure Rock Gym**
Dallas TX
972-732-0307
www.exposurerockclimbing.com

**Texas Rock Gym**
League City TX
281-338-ROCK (281-338-7625)
Houston TX
713-973-ROCK (713-973-7625)
www.texrockgym.com

## Vermont

**Petra Cliffs Climbing Center**
Burlington VT
802-65- PETRA (802-657-3872)
www.petracliffs.com

## Virginia

**Sportrock Climbing Center**
Alexandria VA
703-212-ROCK (703-212-7625)
www.sportrock.com

**Peak Experiences**
Providence Forge VA
804-966-1941

## Washington

**Stone Gardens**
Seattle WA
206-781-9828
www.stonegardens.com

## Wisconsin

**Vertical Stronghold
   Climbing Gym**
Appleton WI

**Adventure Rock
   Climbing Gym**
Brookfield WI
414-790-6800
E-mail: adventurerock@
   juno.com

**Boulders**
Madison WI

**Solid Rock Sports**
Milwaukee WI
414-288-9946

**Vertical Reality Wisconsin**
Whitewater WI

## Wyoming

**Cody Rock Gym**
Cody WY
307-587-5222
www.nmfiber.com/~codyrockgym

**Teton Rock Gym**
Jackson WY
307-733-0707

## Canada

**Off the Wall Rock Climbing**
Barrie ON
705-727-1161
E-mail: offwall@
   offthewalclimbing.on.ca
www.offthewallclimbing.on.ca

**Horizon Roc Climbing Centre**
Montreal PQ
www.cam.org/~roc

**Gravity Climbing Club**
Nelson BC
250-352-6125
www.gravityclimbingclub.com

**The Edge Climbing Center**
North Vancouver BC

**Roc's Nest**
Petawawa ON
613-687-2932

**Vicks Vertical Walls**
Saskatoon SK

**Funky Monkey**
Thunder Bay ON
807-343-0222

# Index